Product Idea to Product Success

A Complete Step-by-Step Guide to Making Money from Your Idea

Matthew Yubas

Broadword Publishing
166 London Court
Cardiff, NJ 08234

Published by Broadword Publishing
166 London Court
Cardiff, NJ 08234

For information about placing an order, please visit:
www.Broadword.com

ISBN: 0-9725521-0-3

Library of Congress Control Number: 2003111239

Printed in the United States of America

10 9 8 7 6 5 4 3

This publication is designed to provide accurate and
authoritative information with regard to the subject matter
covered. It is sold with the understanding that the author and
publisher are not engaged in rendering legal, accounting, or
other professional service.

This product is not a substitute for legal advice.

Cover design by Synapz, Inc.
Edited by Meredith Gould, Ph.D.

Contents

Acknowledgements

I owe a debt of gratitude to those who contributed to the creation of *Product Idea to Product Success*. Whether it was help with content or moral support, your influence has made the difficult task of writing a book much easier. Thank you to:

My weekly writers group consisting of Sheri McGregor, Lori Hall-McNary, and Julie Wininger who have made a considerable impact on improving my writing skills.

James S. Burns, Ph.D., Eric Chriss, Thomas Cook, Miguel Cubillas, John Drummond, Patrick Hamilton, Tomasz Johannsen, Ken Krohn, JD, Mike Lee, Wayne Lundberg, Doug McDonald, Steve Moschak, Michelle Nguyen, Evelyn Rabin, Ph.D., Becki Rios, Omar Rosalis, Frank Scavo, Bob Soltus, JD, Peter Vigil, and Ken Warburton who provided praiseworthy subject matter suggestions and advice.

Robert Goodman, Ph.D., Mona Klausing, Jimmy Long, and Jon Saltz whose expertise contributed to the design, layout, and flow of this book.

Marisol Bardoneschi, Robert Campbell, Ari Galper, Rod Gullo, Ken Clark, Avrum Topel, Norma White, Robin White, Ann Wuttke, Win Wuttke, Alan Yubas, and Diane Yubas for numerous suggestions and support.

Judy Cullins, Meredith Gould, Ph.D., and Dan Poynter who helped with superior editing and overall writing guidance.

Andrew Chapman, Laurie Gibson, and Evan Yubas for outstanding proofreading and recommendations.

Introduction

Innovation is a cornerstone to long-term economic survival. Every day, newspaper headlines, magazine articles, and academic manuscripts report how new products lead to financial success.

Far too many great ideas go untapped because people come up with inventions and don't know what to do next. These ideas can be both profitable and beneficial to our society, but few ever see the light of day.

I grew up a frustrated inventor. As a child, I collected radios and televisions dumped as trash, brought them up into my lab – our attic – and took them apart. My experiments would often blackout the house. I'm lucky I didn't electrocute myself. I later went on to study electronics engineering to figure out what I had been tinkering with. Now, with a college degree I could unleash my inventions onto the world. So I thought.

You mean I have to market and sell these things? I have great ideas, why can't everyone see that? How do I raise money to pay for prototypes and advertising? I was now an even more frustrated inventor, so I decided to learn about business.

I worked for startups as well as Fortune 500 companies and launched software and communications products. Then I started two companies and learned more about marketing and sales. Today, I help individuals and companies launch products and grow sales with consulting and seminars.

I find that people work very hard and don't always have much to show for it. During the mid-twentieth century, a single income could easily provide for a family of four. By the end of that century a double income was required, leading to both parents having to work and children being raised by outside caregivers. It's entirely possible that a triple income will be needed to support a family of four in the future. To produce a triple income, each spouse would have a full-time job and have a part-time job or side business to keep up. That's too much!

Look around your neighborhood and you'll notice that the people who have an advantage usually own a business, have an advanced degree, or are entrepreneurs. Layoffs and downsizing are a fact of corporate life. Long-term employment is never guaranteed. Therefore, it's helpful to have a side business or royalty income. Now is the time to turn your idea into something real. You'll never know what it will lead to until you try.

Who This Book Is For

This book is about helping people beat the odds. It's about using a systematic process to create and market products. Many people will come up with an idea and then say, "Okay, I have this idea, what can I do with it?" This book answers that question to help you develop your ideas into successful products. All you need is a coach to guide and educate you, similar to a sports coach who teaches players the moves and then encourages and motivates them.

If you're an entrepreneur, inventor, an idea person, or business intending to bring new products and services to market, this book is for you.

In my experience, businesses often do not have a specific process, or there are differences of opinion about what works best. Without a clear process, wasteful redundancies and gaps often occur. A playbook or guide is needed that everyone agrees upon. *Product Idea to Product Success* is that guide. You may adopt all or part of the framework I've offered here so that you can launch your product efficiently and effectively.

Organization of the Book

Product Idea to Product Success begins with three methods to develop and enhance new ideas. You'll learn ways to be creative and how you might enhance your invention.

Do you want to bring your idea to market or license it? The Roadmap chapter will provide directions about using this book to accomplish both.

How do you target customers? What are they looking for in a product? In the How Your Customer Thinks chapter, you'll learn how customers think, how they buy, and how to identify what they want.

The essence of the book is the **Market-Step** process. The **Market-Step** process integrates marketing and sales with the technical aspects of developing your idea into a successful product. There are six steps of the **Market-Step** process. Each step includes diagrams, descriptions, examples, and exercises. While reading this book, you'll have an opportunity to flesh out your idea, test your idea, refine it, plan its future, develop it, and then make money from it.

The Appendices contain advanced details to help you with competition, selecting a target market, raising money and business startup. In addition, there's a framework for writing a detailed product plan.

I've provided Internet resources throughout the book to point you to additional information. You can find even more resources on the Links page of my updated website (www.MattYubas.com). Remember, I'm your coach. For questions and comments, please feel free to send personal email to me at info@MattYubas.com.

Best of luck,

Matthew Yubas

Part One
GETTING STARTED

Hide not your talents, they for use were made. What's a sundial in the shade?

Benjamin Franklin

New Product Ideas
Your Roadmap to Success
Product Failure and Success
Protecting Your Idea
Licensing Your Idea

Chapter 1
New Product Ideas

A mind once stretched by a new idea never regains its original dimension.

Oliver Wendell Holmes Jr.

What do toothbrushes, televisions, can openers, sunglasses, candleholders, tape recorders, and light bulbs have in common? They're all products. But at one point in time, they were unknown until someone invented them – like you. Some inventions are simple and some are complicated. Some inventors actively pursue new ideas, while for others new ideas just come to mind.

Three Approaches to New Ideas

Since you're reading this book, you have an idea you want to turn into a successful product, or maybe you want to come up with a new idea and then develop it. Either way, let me share with you three approaches to creating or enhancing a new product idea. You can:

- Improve existing products
- Uncover problems, needs, and wants
- Look at trends

Improve Existing Products

An invention does not have to be new to world technology. In fact, most new ideas are improvements to existing ideas. An estimated 80% to 90% of United States patents are improvements of some sort over existing patents. (We'll be covering patents in the "Protecting Your Idea" chapter.)

If you want to improve a product, but are not sure how, here's a technique for creating a new product by analyzing an existing one. Perform the following steps to create your product:

1. Ask people who use an existing product how they would like to see it improved.
2. Make a list of each part or feature.
3. Think about how one or more features might be improved.
4. Make feature changes such as adding, removing, substituting, improving, combining, or rearranging.
5. Put this all together to create your new product.

For example, let's examine an electric can opener. There are three major components: the knife, the handle, and the motor that rotates the can. Your innovation might indicate changes such as using a laser instead of a knife to cut into the can, holding the can in place with a clamp instead of using a handle, and instead of cutting by rotating the can, letting the laser move around the perimeter. In this hypothetical example, major components were identified and then redesigned to form a completely new product that functions faster and more efficiently.

Examples of product improvements include an electric toothbrush, which is more effective than a regular toothbrush; a cordless drill, which is more convenient than a corded drill; and the microwave oven, which is faster than either an electric or gas model.

Keep in mind that people sometimes have to be shown they have a need. Until its development, no one was demanding a microwave oven. People were happily cooking with gas or electric ovens. But once they experienced the benefits of faster cooking, the microwave oven became a household necessity.

Another method for creating new products involves taking a product or technology being used for one market and then applying it to another. The remote control for the TV was applied to garage door openers. Suitcases with wheels were good, but became much better with in-line skate wheels. And think about all the products that came to be as a result of the Velcro™ hook and loop fastener.

Uncover Problems, Needs, and Wants

A product idea can come from solving a problem, or satisfying a need or want. Maybe the idea comes from your own needs, or from listening to complaints or requests. People are always looking for ways to do something better, easier, or more cost effectively. An idea can come from a business issue or something at home. A good product idea is one that saves time, offers convenience, saves or makes money, provides safety, offers prestige or social status, or alleviates boredom.

Think about the light bulb, calculator, or paper clip. They were all invented to fill someone's individual need. Now, these products solve problems for the masses.

Look at Trends

Trends in the social, political, economic, technological, or natural environment provide a source of product ideas. Inventions based on trends have a tendency to appeal to people interested in safety, pleasure, comfort, efficiency, or fashion.

For example, large numbers of baby-boomers who have money to spend are looking for products that will induce feelings of youth and energy. Trends in environmental awareness have given rise to products such as air purifiers, radon detectors, and asbestos-free items. People who purchased these products were motivated by health and safety. Products such as spill-proof coffee cups, writing pads that attach to the dashboard, and hands-free cell phone kits emerged as people began doing more in their cars.

What are some of the trends happening right now in your industry, your city, region, state, country, or in the world? And, how can you capitalize on these trends?

Creative Thinking

Whether your idea results from improving an existing product, solving a problem, or observing trends, creativity is at the core. Creativity comes to people in different ways. Some people are creative first thing in the morning or late at night; while taking a shower, listening to music, driving, or shopping; under pressure to perform; or when it's still and quiet. Sometimes you'll have to actively seek creative solutions, while at other times ideas may just pop up into the mind. Or, you may experience a combination of both.

When I need to come up with an idea, I start by writing down questions related to a problem. For some reason, when I read the questions out loud, my brain begins processing. Later, when I'm in more a receptive state, such as first thing in the morning, or when I'm out walking, answers to these questions begin flowing. I make sure I have paper or computer nearby to document my thoughts. I just put my thoughts down and then organize them later.

If you notice you're most creative when you're feeling peaceful, make time in your busy schedule to relax in a quiet place. Take a series of deep breaths to help clear your mind. Have a notebook handy to scribble ideas and diagrams. Don't worry if your ideas make sense, just write them down, and analyze them later.

Brainstorming is a popular technique to stimulate creative thinking. You can do this by yourself, but a small group of people generating ideas is better. Find a place where there are minimal distractions. To get the creative juices flowing, follow these steps:

1. Start by explaining the problem and then posing a question such as, "How can people be more productive while sitting in traffic?" Or, "In an ideal world in which money was no object, how can we make this product better?"

2. Write down any idea that comes to mind while answering the question. In addition, feel free to go off on tangents. Offer new ideas. Build upon the ideas of others. If you can't put your idea into words, draw diagrams, flowcharts, or pictures.
3. If ideas don't seem to flow, try thinking of negative solutions. Ask, "What would *not* work?" Or, "What features would the customer *not* want?"
4. Refrain from evaluating the validity of each idea at this time. Just write them all down and move on to the next.
5. When the flow of ideas comes to an end or a time limit is reached, group similar solutions together. For any negative responses, see if there's a corresponding positive solution. Then ask, "Which are the top three ideas so far?" Score these ideas in terms of advantages and disadvantages to end-users.
6. Now, take the top three ideas and ask, "How can these ideas be made better?" Sleep on that question and come back to it in a day or two. Let your mind work on the solution.
7. When you get back together, agree to which is the best solution out of the top three, and continue to brainstorm more details.

Again, no matter how extravagant the concept is, write it down and worry about refining it later. Most inventors have been told they were crazy and their ideas will never work. I consider that fuel to persevere.

A note of caution: Be clear up-front if you're in a group setting about who owns any of the new ideas being generated. Consider putting in writing either that the members are volunteers, being paid for their time, are exchanging services, or sharing the results of the group effort.

Keep It Simple

Inventions can be very simple. For example, I enjoy eating tuna fish and go through the messy process of squeezing water or oil from the can. While shopping one day, I saw a simple product. At about $2.50, the tuna fish strainer was a no-brainer purchase. This product is simply a round plastic disk the size of a tuna can lid with holes and a handle. It solves the problem of draining tuna quickly, without a mess.

This simple little product was someone's invention. It's straightforward, easy to comprehend, and solves a problem. Your invention does not have to be complicated. Notice how popular products are those that perform one simple function. You probably have many ideas. Start with something that's simple to create and simple to understand.

Market-Step Enhancement

Research and development costs have risen to the point where we cannot prototype and develop ten ideas, hoping one will take off and provide a profit. We need to turn ideas into marketable products using a systematic and responsible process that will yield more successes and screen out possible failures at the outset. The method to turn your ideas into successful products is called the **Market-Step**™ process.

The **Market-Step** process starts with the idea stage. We'll look at your product idea in terms of its advantages over the competition, customer benefits, and potential profit. In addition, we'll look at potential government regulations and industry certification approvals. And, I'll show you a simple method to get a reality check on your product idea. The **Market-Step** process is designed to get you thinking from many perspectives by answering a series of questions, including:

- Who will buy my product?
- How much are they willing to spend?
- Where will they buy it?

- Is the need for this type of product growing?
- Is the competition fierce?
- Can my product offer a competitive advantage?
- How much will my product cost to make?
- Who can I get to produce my product?
- How will my product be marketed?

Answering these types of questions first will allow you to develop your product from a customer and market perspective. In other words, your product will stand a better chance of being sellable and profitable. Don't worry. I'll lead you through the process one step at a time.

Chapter 2
Your Roadmap to Success

There is no prescribed route to follow to arrive at a new idea. You have to make the intuitive leap. But the difference is that once you've made that intuitive leap you have to justify it by filling in the intermediate steps.

Stephen Hawking

Michelangelo once said that his statue of David was embedded in the block of marble and he merely chipped away the edges to reveal it. Is your product idea inside your mind just waiting to come alive? Or, is your product already formed and you need only to smooth out the edges?

I'll walk you through the process with a series of discussions, examples, and exercises. In this hands-on book, your idea will come to life as we progress. The **Market-Step** process will take you through the following steps from idea to launch:

1. Self-Evaluation
2. Concept Evaluation
3. Prototype Evaluation
4. Product and Market Planning
5. Product Development and Marketing Tactics
6. Product Launch, Marketing and Selling

The following is an overview of the key steps to making your idea a reality. Please use this roadmap as a navigational tool to guide and monitor your progress.

The Steps from Product Idea to Product Success

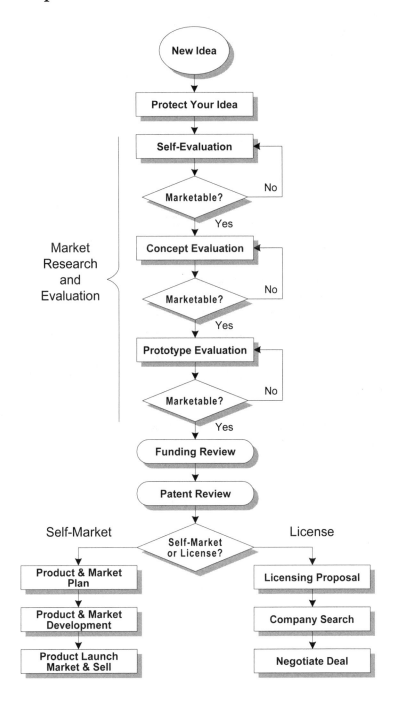

Getting Started

❑ **Protect Your Idea (Chapter 4)**

When you have an idea, you need to protect it. The first line of defense is to set the date of conception. Start by documenting your idea in an inventor's notebook, but don't file a patent until you evaluate its marketability.

Market Research and Evaluation

❑ **Self-Evaluation (Chapter 9)**

Start the **Market-Step** process by evaluating your product idea's marketability. Your product idea is marketable if and when it solves a problem, meets a need or want, overcomes competition, and generates a profit.

❑ **Concept Evaluation (Chapter 11)**

The second step of the **Market-Step** process is to determine if people like the concept of your product idea. To test your invention, you'll need to uncover which people or companies are your future customers. After identifying potential customers, ask them to evaluate how well your product idea solves a problem, or meets a need or want.

❑ **Prototype Evaluation (Chapter 12)**

The third is detailed evaluation by giving people a prototype to examine. A prototype is a working model that looks, feels, and functions similarly to the finished product. I'll lead you through the process of creating a prototype that resembles what your customer wants. Then, I'll show you how to get detailed feedback by interviewing potential customers.

❑ **Funding Your Idea (Appendix F)**

Do you need to raise money to develop and market your product? Initially, you'll need money for expenses such as market research, equipment, and prototype development. Raising money is a normal part of doing business when you start, grow, and expand.

❑ **Patent Review (Chapter 13)**
You performed a preliminary patent search earlier. Now it's worth your time and money to perform a detailed patent search and possibly file for a patent.

❑ **Self-Market or License (Chapter 14)**
What do you do with your new product? Your choices are to either self-market or license it. In some cases you can do both or sell the rights. Self-marketing means turning your idea into a marketable product that you intend to sell directly to an end-user, and/or through a distributor or retailer. Under a licensing agreement, a business will produce and sell your product in exchange for royalties.

Path A: Self-Market Development

If you've decided to self-market, follow the remaining steps on Path A. If you've decided to license your idea, see the next section for Path B.

❑ **Product and Market Plan (Chapter 15)**
Plan your work and then work your plan. The fourth step of the **Market-Step** process involves planning product design and marketing programs. Product design results from combining your innovation with needs and wants you've discovered through research. Market planning involves positioning, pricing, and communications.

❑ **Product and Market Development (Chapter 16)**
In the fifth step you'll develop your product in stages (i.e., alpha, beta, commercial release). You'll use the beta product to obtain feedback to confirm functionality and eliminate bugs before final production.

❑ **Product Launch, Market and Sell (Chapter 17)**
In the sixth step you're ready to move into production and launch your product. This is the most exciting part of your

project. You've given birth to your idea and are bringing it out into the world. And as you would with a child, you'll need to nurture and grow your product, with marketing and sales strategies and tactics.

Path B: Licensing

You've determined that licensing is for you. Follow the steps in Path B to license your product idea.

❑ **Licensing Proposal (Chapter 5)**
Before approaching a company or product agent, organize your marketing research into a proposal. Some companies have their own forms to fill out; others ask to submit in your own format.

If you feel comfortable presenting and negotiating, seek companies on your own to license your product. Otherwise, find product agents who will seek companies and negotiate on your behalf.

If the company likes what you have, you'll then negotiate a licensing agreement, then carry out the obligations, and collect royalties.

Going Forward

Now that you have an overview of the steps from product idea to product success, we'll start with some background information. Then, we'll go through the **Market-Step** process, one step at a time.

Chapter 3
Product Failure and Success

Entrepreneurs are risk-takers, willing to roll the dice with their money or reputations on the line in support of an idea or enterprise. They willingly assume responsibility for the success or failure of a venture and are answerable for all its facets.

Victor Kiam

What Is a Product?

A product can be any tangible or intangible object or service. Your tangible product might be a new type of hammer, toaster, or electronic circuit board. An intangible product is something you can't hold in your hands and would include things like software products, web sites, publishing content, and any service.

Activities for developing tangible products are similar to those used for intangible products. For example, if you intend to sell sports content on the web, you must uncover the specific need or want, review market trends, determine a target market, discover competitive threats, understand buyer behavior, and so on. The same approach holds for any tangible product idea, such as a new handheld communications device.

Any tangible and intangible product or service will be identified as a **Product** in this book. The concepts in this book apply to products as well as services.

Why Do Products Fail?

We don't intentionally plan for failure; we just fail to plan. That's how the saying goes. We all believe we're doing the best we can to improve chances for product success. Some causes for failure are within our domain and some are not. While companies may blame the economy for product failure, failure is more likely the result of misjudging the customer and/or inefficient management systems.

This book will show you how to overcome these pitfalls and keep you on course for success. The following are the key reasons for product failures in the marketplace. See if you can identify with any of these.

- Not thinking about the customer, marketing, and sales before development begins
- Not getting feedback from potential customers
- Not understanding the buying process of the customer
- Not determining the product costs and selling price before development
- No method for evaluating new ideas
- Not protecting your idea
- Obtaining a patent before determining the marketability of your invention
- Designing a product without performing a patent search for potential infringement
- Waiting more than a year after public disclosure to file a patent
- Not putting your plans in writing
- Trying to do it all yourself
- Designing a product without considering manufacturability
- Not considering the competition when developing, pricing, and marketing your product
- Developing a product with only the needs of a few people in mind
- Not following a sequence of steps
- Lack of consistent message to the customer from marketing, promotions, and sales
- No planning for a product launch
- Personal goals override company goals

Why Do Products Succeed?

What factors determine product success? For one thing, avoid the pitfalls mentioned above. But it is important to know that successful products:

- Solve a problem or satisfy a need or want
- Include great packaging
- Present stylish design
- Are available where the target market shops
- Are priced accordingly
- Offer a risk-free guarantee

In addition to having the right product, the company behind the product:

- Is easy to do business with
- Has a process to generate and screen new ideas
- Begins the new idea process by identifying customer problems and needs
- Has sufficient funding in place
- Has one person who maintains the product vision and manages the project
- Has a work environment that's fun and exciting

Knowing what fails and what succeeds provides important information. You do not need to reinvent the wheel. Following the steps in this book will increase your odds of success. Keep in mind that the technically superior product does not always win. Of course, the product must be sufficient to meet the needs of the customer. But there is more to it than just the product. The customer is looking for a variety of things including practical functionality, consistent quality, reasonable pricing, style, an identifiable image, and customer service from a company that appears stable and in it for the long term.

Chapter 4
Protecting Your Idea

Because ideas have to be original only with regard to their adaptation to the problem at hand, I am always interested in novel ideas others have used successfully.

Thomas A. Edison

Before spending thousands of dollars on a patent, you'll want to make sure your product idea is marketable and commercially viable. It would not be cost-effective to patent every product idea you have.

Once you file a patent, product details are open to the public to review. Products like WD-40™ and Coca-Cola™ were not patented because these companies know that patent filing will disclose their product secrets to the world. Unfortunately, some unscrupulous people review patents for the sole purpose of stealing ideas. They can take your idea, make a few changes, and call it their own. Also, a large company with a staff of attorneys can find a way to beat you up in court. In the 1980s, I filed a patent for an improved telephone answering machine. An electronics company (whose name begins with "S") filed a patent for a similar device shortly afterwards. They said, in essence, that I had no hope of beating them in court, so I dropped it.

If your idea is a "secret recipe" and difficult for others to replicate, then you might not want to file a patent. Also, if your idea is a fad that might fade in a year, you probably don't need to file a patent. But, you never know how long fads or technology trends can last. When the first photocopy machine was invented, people asked, "Why would anyone need to photocopy something?"

The United States Patent and Trademark Office (USPTO) grants patents to help advance technology. A patent gives you the right to exclude others. But, a patent does *not* give you the right to produce and sell your invention.

Keep in mind that patents do not infringe on patents. Products infringe on patents. It's therefore possible that your product, built to the specifications of your patent, may infringe on another patent. In fact, the patent office will search for potential infringement before granting a patent, but is not responsible for uncovering conflicting claims. In the event of infringement, the final authority to validate a patent is the court system.

At the design stage, your invention must take into consideration existing patents. In simple terms, you'll need to make sure your product does not include all the claims of any one patent. For example, if a patent claims to do A, B, and C, your product cannot include all of the same. You could claim your product does A, B, and D. But, you cannot claim your product does A, B, C, and D, because it includes all of A, B, and C.

To prevent someone from designing around your patent, you might need to file several patents to cover variations. For example, Epson has many patents on its ink jet technology. Their ink jet print head is unique, so Epson filed several patents to cover a range of technological variations. As a result, they were able to prevent companies such as HP from making a similar ink jet printer. But, that didn't stop HP from coming up with their own design with the same function using different technology.

So why do you need a patent? While you do not need a patent to market your product, a patent can give you a competitive advantage. Patents add value to your business. The patent becomes intellectual property and can be considered a valuable asset, in part because it can prevent others from producing a similar product.

If you want to license your product, seeking a patent makes sense. Before any business negotiates licensing, your invention must be patented or in a patent pending state. File for a patent after your market research demonstrates a need for your product, and you've worked the numbers to show that you can generate a profit.

Over six-and-a-half million patents have been issued since the first one in 1790. To determine if your invention is patentable, the USPTO looks at patent applications that are novel, non-obvious, and are either a new process (e.g., converting gold into jewelry), a new machine or device (e.g., motor), a new composition of matter (e.g., chemical), or an improvement on an existing patent. You can't submit just a theory, but it must be something that works in real life. In essence, a patent can be anything that is humanly produced.

Ideas that are not patentable include mathematical formulas (e.g., c = a+b), laws of nature (e.g., gravity), and naturally occurring substances (e.g., sun, gold, wood). What *is* patentable is a unique process for converting sunlight into electricity, processing gold into jewelry, or transforming wood into paper.

Before discussing your idea with anyone such as an investor or prototype maker, have him or her sign a non-disclosure agreement (NDA). When someone signs an NDA, that person agrees to keep your idea confidential. An NDA signals that you're serious about protecting your idea and that you will take legal recourse. To understand what an NDA entails, see the Non-Disclosure Agreement in Appendix G. But, I suggest you discuss creating an NDA with an attorney.

The First to Conceive Wins

In the rest of the world, the first to file gets the patent. In the United States, the first to *conceive the idea* gets the patent. And so, you must document your idea as soon as you come up with it. If someone else comes up with the same idea, you want to prove that you conceived of it first. In the United States, there are four ways to document the conception of your idea:

- Record your idea in an Idea Notebook
- File a Document Disclosure
- File a Provisional Patent
- File a Utility, Design, or Plant Patent

If there's a conflict over who came up with an idea first, the Patent Office will look at documents that show a date of conception. In addition, they will examine if the idea is being made into a real product. This is referred to as "reduction to practice." For example, let's assume two people came up with an idea at roughly the same time. They both documented the idea in a notebook. One person is actively working on turning the invention into a product and the other person is not. In this case, the Patent Office will likely award the patent to the person who is in pursuit of developing and marketing the invention.

The One-Year Rule

If you intend to file a patent, be aware that if you make your product idea public, you'll have one year to file for a patent. The one-year rule allows you to test market your invention before you need to file a patent. The one-year rule, imposed by the Patent Office, says that you must file for any type of patent within one year if any of the following events occur:

- Any public use of your invention in the United States
- Actual sale of your invention in the United States
- An offer to sell your invention in the United States
- Descriptions appear in a published document anywhere in the world

If you do not file for a patent within one year after one of these events occurs, your invention will become public domain and unpatentable.

Your Idea Notebook

Your Idea Notebook, also called an Inventor's Logbook, is an important place to record your idea. A thorough idea notebook documents the conception date, as well as the details of your idea.

Use a bound notebook with numbered pages. The notebook binding should be stitched so that pages cannot be added or easily removed. Write entries in ink and do not erase mistakes, just cross them out. Write on every consecutive page and don't skip pages. Here are the things to record:

- Describe your idea
- Describe how you came up with the idea
- Provide sketches and drawings to clarify your idea (you may also attach papers such as computer printouts and photos with permanent glue)
- List all parts and materials needed to turn your idea into a product
- Describe problems you've had and how you solved them
- Indicate marketing and sales ideas

Sign and date all pages when they're created and have them signed and dated by a non-family member witness who has no financial interest in your invention, but has some knowledge of the subject matter.

Disclosure Document Program

The Disclosure Document Program is another way to set the date of conception of your idea. It's useful if you choose not to show your idea to anyone else. Other than using an Idea Notebook, this is the least expensive way to record a conception date. The Patent Office will preserve the disclosure for two years, but this disclosure is not a patent application, nor does it provide patent pending status. To file a Disclosure Document, you must provide a clear and complete explanation of the manner and process for making and using your invention. Your description must have sufficient detail to enable a person with ordinary knowledge in the relevant field to make and use the product. When the nature of the invention permits, a drawing or sketch ould be included.

When the Patent Office receives your Disclosure Document, it does not examine your idea, but merely holds it and provides you with a date of its receipt. You'll need the following for a Disclosure Document application:

- Cover Sheet (PTO/SB/95), or provide your own cover letter that states, "The undersigned, being the inventor of the disclosed invention, requests that the enclosed papers be accepted under the Disclosure Document Program, and that they be preserved for a period of two years."
- A description and drawing of your idea printed on your letterhead in 8 ½ x 11 inch or A4 format
- $10 Filing Fee

Types of Patents

The are three general types of patents issued by the U.S. Patent and Trademark Office: 1) Utility Patent, 2) Design Patent, and 3) Plant Patent.

Utility Patent

When people use the term "patent" they're usually referring to a Utility Patent. The Utility Patent is the most common of all patent types. A Utility Patent protects an idea – how it works or how it's used. The protection lasts for 20 years from the date the application is filed. Utility Patents are issued for a new process, a new machine, a new composition of matter, or an improvement on an existing patent. Examples include computers, cameras, cell phones, toasters, and thousands of other ideas. This is the minimum you'll need to file for a Utility Patent application:

- Utility Patent Application (Form PTO/SB/05)
- Fee Transmittal (Form PTO/SB/17)
- Declaration (Form PTO/SB/01)

- Application Data Sheet (applicant information, see 37 CFR 1.76)
- Specification (title, background of idea, description)
- Drawings
- $375 Filing Fee

Design Patent

A Design Patent protects the visual and ornamental appearance of an object but not its functional aspects. It protects the shape, pattern, and surface look. For example, a Design Patent can protect a non-functional aspect of a functional product such as the shape of a cell phone. The protection lasts for 14 years from the date the patent is issued (this is different from a Utility Patent). Examples include the shape of a Corvette car body, the shape of a Tiffany lamp, or the look of a Rolex watch. This is the minimum you'll need to file for a Design Patent application:

- Design Patent Application (Form PTO/SB/18)
- Fee Transmittal (Form PTO/SB/17)
- Declaration (Form PTO/SB/01)
- Application Data Sheet (applicant information, see 37 CFR 1.76)
- Specification (title of the design, and a brief description of the nature and intended use of the article in which the design is embodied)
- Drawings or photographs
- Description of the figure(s) of the drawing
- $165 Filing Fee

Plant Patent

A Plant Patent protects novel and non-obvious reproducible varieties of plants (e.g., roses, orchids, tulips). The plant must be living, have a single genetic makeup, and duplicated through asexual reproduction. The protection lasts for 20 years from the date the application is filed. The Patent Office recommends that you contact them before filing a Plant Patent. This is the minimum you'll need to file for a Plant Patent application:

- Plant Patent Application (Form PTO/SB/19)
- Fee Transmittal (Form PTO/SB/17)
- Declaration (Form PTO/SB/01)
- Application Data Sheet (applicant information, see 37 CFR 1.76)
- Specification (title, genus and species, variety, description)
- Drawings
- Oath or Declaration
- $260 Filing Fee

Costs of Patents

Although you may file a patent application yourself, I recommend using a patent attorney for accuracy and time savings. Attorney fees for a patent search and filing often start at $5,000. The cost of patenting your invention will also include a Filing Fee, sent at the time of application, and an Issue Fee, that's due when the patent is approved. In addition, there are Maintenance Fees for Utility Patents to keep your patent enforced from the date it's granted. The following list of fees for the year 2003, apply to individuals and organizations with fewer than 500 employees. For organizations with 500 or more employees, fees are doubled.

Utility Patent Basic Fees

- Filing Fee: $375
- Issue Fee when patent is granted: $650
- Maintenance Fee due by three years and six months after the grant date: $445
- Maintenance Fee due by seven years and six months after the grant date: $1,025
- Maintenance Fee due by eleven years and six months after the grant date: $1,575

Design Patent Basic Fees

- Filing Fee: $165
- Issue Fee when patent is granted: $235
- No Maintenance Fee

Plant Patent Basic Fees

- Filing Fee: $260
- Issue Fee when patent is granted: $315
- No Maintenance Fee

After an application is filed and the patent examiner believes everything is in order, you'll receive a Notice of Allowance. The next step is for you to pay the Issue Fee. Once the Issue Fee is paid, the patent is known as "Issued" which means the patent is now yours.

Provisional Patents

A Provisional Patent gives you the opportunity to extend the time before you file a Utility Patent. If you've displayed your product in public and the one-year window is about to close, you can file a Provisional Patent to give you an extra year to file for a Utility Patent. In addition, a Provisional Patent sets the date you conceived the idea as a backup to your invention notebook. It also allows you a quick method to designate your idea with the Patent Pending notice.

The Provisional Patent does not later automatically become a Utility Patent and it cannot be renewed. You must still file for a Utility Patent. Keep in mind that anything new that you claim later in your Utility Patent application, the date of conception is set as of the Utility Patent application date rather than the Provisional Patent date. This means that if there is an infringement case, the date of infringement is set as of the Utility Patent date.

If you file a Provisional Patent, the Patent Office records your idea but doesn't check to see if there's a conflict with existing patents. A Provisional Patent gives you time to test market your idea and then determine that your idea is worth the time and expense to file a patent. This is the minimum you'll need to file for a Provisional Patent application:

- Provisional Patent Cover Sheet (Form PTO/SB/16)
- Description of your idea
- Drawings that describe your idea
- $80 Filing Fee
- Optionally include a self-addressed, stamped postcard that the USPTO will mark and mail to you showing the date received. Indicate on the back of the postcard "Provisional Patent," the invention title, a list of contents (description and drawings) and the number of pages

Preliminary Patent Search

Before starting the process of designing, testing, and producing your product, you'll need to see if patents exist that are similar to your invention. Search for patents at the United States Patent and Trademark Office website (www.uspto.gov). The search is free and simple. Click on the link for a patent search. Enter keywords related to your product. For example, if your product idea was for a new electronic organizer, you'd enter the keyword "organizer" to start. You'll be presented with a list of patent titles. Click on a title to see the patent holder, abstract (overview), similar patents referenced by the patent examiner, claims, and description.

If the patent looks similar to your idea, write down its number. Remember, though, that even if a patent is similar to yours, it's still possible to get a patent. When in doubt, ask for patent search assistance from a patent attorney. It might save you some money if you present a patent attorney with a list of patents that seem similar to yours. See Chapter 13 for more details about patent searching.

For software patents, search the Software Patent Institute database website (www.spi.org).

Where to Find Patent Attorneys

Talk with other inventors and entrepreneurs to discover rec-
ommended patent attorneys. You can also find patent attorneys
in the Yellow Pages, or by searching the Patent Office website
(www.uspto.gov/web/offices/dcom/olia/oed/roster/)   for   registered patent attorneys in your area.

Talk to a number of patent attorneys to find out if they have
experience with your product type. Ask at what stage of the development process should you file a patent. I give them good
marks if they say, "After you determine marketability."

International Patents

Let's assume that your idea has universal appeal and would include markets outside the United States. If this is the case, you'll
need to file an international patent. Recently passed international patent treaties now make it possible to file one international patent for a number of countries. This is a complex area,
so seek patent attorney counsel. In the meantime, you can get
information on international patents through the following web
sites:

- Patent Cooperation Treaty
  (www.uspto.gov/web/offices/pac/dapps/pct/)
- World Intellectual Property Organization
  (www.wipo.org)
- European Patent Office
  (www.european-patent-office.org)

An international patent must be filed within one year of filing a United States Utility, Design, Plant, or Provisional Patent.
An international patent must also be filed *before* an invention is
placed before the public, such as at a trade show. Companies
that have an unpatented product and an upcoming trade show,
will often file a quick Provisional Patent before the show to get a
year to a file for an international patent.

Trademark Protection

Trademarks play a valuable role in marketing your products. Think of trademarks as the legal aspect of branding. A trademarked product helps build trust, reputation, and loyalty. Whenever you see a trademarked product from Sony, Hershey Foods, or General Electric, you intuitively know what you're getting before ever opening the package. A trademarked brand name allows a company to distinguish itself and prevent others from using a similar name that may tarnish its good reputation. As a result, trademarks are valuable company assets. If trademarks did not exist, inferior products could be advertised by a company called General Electrical and consumers would likely be confused about which products are the real ones from General Electric.

A trademark must be distinctive and not a common word or phrase. A trademark may consist of a word, letter, number, symbol (logo), color, shape, or combination of these. In some instances, distinctive sounds and smells can be trademarked. A trademark will help you:

- Add value to your product brand and business
- Keep competitors from copying your brand name
- Protect your product's reputation

If your product is trademarked, you can prevent others from using the same or similar names. In particular, there should be no confusion between a trademarked name and another product. For example, the product "Krazy Glue" is trademarked. If you advertised your product as "Krazi Glue" or "Crazy Goo" you'd probably get a "cease and desist" letter from the trademark's owner, because your product name will confuse consumers. For an easy test, say the words out loud. If the name you've chosen sounds like a trademark, you're most likely facing an infringement. Ultimately, the decision of infringement and damages lies in the courtroom.

Another test in determining if your trademark application is acceptable is that it should not dilute an existing trademarked brand's reputation. For example, Sony has a trademark on its Walkman portable electronics products. If a new pet product was called the Dog-Walkman, not only would there be a cause for concern about confusion, but Sony might not want to be associated with a pet product.

Filing a Trademark

Before filing, the trademark must be "in use." In use means that you must display the product name with the trademark symbol on a flyer, website, or product label to the public. Adding a "TM" symbol to your product name (e.g., Productname™) puts the world on notice that you claim rights to that name. Use the trademark in your advertising, brochures, flyers, labels, t-shirts, or on your website.

To obtain a federal registered trademark, you'll need to file with the U.S. Patent and Trademark Office. The registration process is now performed online (www.uspto.gov) with the Trademark Electronic Application System (TEAS). Once a federal trademark is granted, you may use the symbol "R" inside a circle (e.g., Productname®).

The federal trademark filing fee is currently $335. The trademark lasts for ten years. But may be renewed for additional ten-year periods as long as the trademark is in use. A registered trademark makes it easier to sue for damages in the event of infringement. In addition, a registered trademark will give you the right to obtain a website domain address with the same name. Internet law is still in flux and this may change.

Keep in mind that in the United States, trademark ownership is usually granted to the first to use the mark, rather than first to file. I suggest that once you come up with a product name, add the "TM" symbol and display it on a website or printed materials. Once you're able to determine that your product is marketable, officially file for a trademark.

Your other option involves filing for an "Intent to Use" trademark for $100. This is helpful to reserve a trademark in the future while having nothing in-use at this time. As part of the process, you must sign a sworn statement that you have a real intention to use the trademark. When your product is ready, you'll still need to put the trademark in-use and then file an application.

To obtain a trademark for your business name (known as a "Service Mark"), you'll need to file with your state's Secretary of State. In addition, if your company name is unique and you're doing business in more than one state, you are advised to also register for a federal trademark. A service mark can also protect an event such as the Olympic Games, which has the five rings trademarked.

Search to Avoid Infringement

To perform a trademark search on your product name, go to the U.S. Patent and Trademark Office website (www.uspto.gov) and select "trademarks." Enter the product name you have in mind and see if it exists. In addition, use search engines such as Google or AltaVista to see if the product name exists.

The key is to make sure that your product name would not be confused with any existing trademarks. If your product name sounds or looks similar to the name of an existing trademark, you could be challenged.

Once you own a trademark, it's up to you to monitor for infringement. I suggest doing that on a monthly basis by searching the Internet for products using your product name. If a potential trademark infringement exists, talk to an attorney who specializes in intellectual property.

Copyright Protection

Original artistic expressions that you create are automatically protected under the U.S. copyright laws. Work protected includes books, presentations, poetry, websites, software code, recordings, and photographs. You do not need to register to have protection. Copyright law automatically protects your artistic expression. But, you'll need to show ownership.

To show ownership, provide a notice on your work. The copyright notice format is a "C" inside a circle, the word "Copyright" or the abbreviation 'Copr.' followed by the year the work was created, and its owner (your name or company name). For example, a copyright notice can be displayed as:

© 2003 Company. All rights reserved.

The phrase "All rights reserved" is not necessarily required. It is a leftover from old laws but still common practice.

I suggest registering your work as soon as your creation is completed. To enforce the copyright and sue for damages, you need to file with the United States Library of Congress. Go to their website (www.loc.gov), click on copyrights, and then download Form TX for written text (e.g., books, software, user manuals, websites), Form VA for visual arts, Form PA for performing arts, Form SE for periodical serials (e.g., journals, magazines, newsletters), and Form SR for sound recordings. Fill out the form and submit the application with a sample of your work. The current fee is $30. Registration becomes effective as of the date the copyright office receives your application, fee, and sample.

The copyright lasts for your personal lifetime plus 70 years. The number of allowable years past a lifetime is currently under debate. One trick to extending copyright life is by listing a grandchild as co-author. This would extend copyright protection to include the longer life of the grandparent or grandchild. For works made for hire, the copyright lasts for 95 years from publication, or 120 years from creation, whichever is shorter.

Chapter 5
Licensing Your Idea

Some day I hope to write a book where the royalties will pay for the copies I give away.

Clarence Darrow

What is licensing as it relates to inventions? Licensing is giving a company permission to manufacture, distribute, and sell a product based on your idea. In exchange, you'll receive payments known as royalties. You are the licensor and the company is the licensee.

For example, let's suppose I came up with an idea for a new toy. I evaluated the product idea against similar existing products and concluded mine was better. I made a list of parts and looked up the costs in a parts catalog. I used competitor retail prices as my selling price. Then, I estimated expenses and calculated a profit potential. Since the profit potential looked reasonable, I continued with my evaluations. Next, I surveyed people about how well my product idea solved a problem (providing entertainment). More than 80% of the fifty people I showed it to liked the solution (toy). I built a rough prototype and showed it to another fifty people. Again, more than 80% of the people liked it and offered suggestions.

I had no interest in running a toy business, so I searched the Internet for reputable companies that manufactured and sold toys. I let them know I had a new product that received positive feedback. They suggested I submit a proposal. The proposal included a description of the idea, the benefits it offered over the competition, survey results, and a profit potential. The company liked it and wanted to meet me. At the meeting, I talked about how the product received positive feedback, the profit potential, and the royalties I was looking for. After many discussions, we arrived at a Licensing Agreement.

The Licensing Process

Before approaching a company to license your idea, you'll need to do some homework. Think about licensing from the company's point of view. They get flooded with requests to license products and don't have time to perform initial assessments on every product idea. They want to see marketability test results, manufacturing costs, and profit projections. In almost all cases, your product idea must be patented or patent pending before a company will talk with you.

The **Market-Step** process outlined in the following chapters will lead you through the marketing research you'll need to prepare the information that licensing companies want. Use the following steps to license your product idea:

1. Perform market research and evaluate your idea in terms of profit potential, competition, and market acceptance.
2. File a patent and receive a patent pending designation. While waiting for the outcome of the patent filing, continue with the following steps.
3. Write a licensing proposal.
4. Search for companies that might license your product idea.
5. Make a personal contact inside a company and send an introductory letter with a general product description, product benefits, and your background and credentials.
6. If the company likes your introductory letter, both you and company representatives should meet to sign a mutual non-disclosure agreement. This covers confidential information that the company may divulge, and your information such as marketing and financial statements.
7. Send a licensing proposal to the company.

8. The company makes an evaluation (e.g., financial return, manufacturability, and distribution).
9. If the company is interested, you'll discuss licensing terms and reach an oral agreement.
10. The company generates a license agreement for you to review and sign.
11. You and the company carry out the terms of the license agreement.

These licensing steps may seem straightforward, but plan on going through several iterations to find the right company, and then additional iterations to negotiate and agree to terms. I advise hiring an attorney, experienced in licensing, to review any contracts and represent you in negotiations.

During the evaluation period, the company might want to see a prototype. A prototype might be a physical working model, or it could be computer-aided design or simulation. In some cases, an acceptable prototype is a very detailed artist's illustration. Ask the company what's required. If developing the prototype is expensive, ask if they'd contribute to the cost.

What Do Companies Want?

Companies look for signs that a product will make money and is a fit with their product line. Your product might not be a fit for one company, but could be perfect for another. In general, companies want a product that:

- **Will make a profit** – Companies want products that produce profits inline with their business. For example, a company such as Sony needs products that produce hundreds of thousands or millions of dollars in profit. A small or medium size company might be happy with a product that produces fifty thousand dollars in profit.
- **Is patented or patent pending** – Companies fear being sued by inventors who claim their ideas were stolen. In addition, they want a unique product that's protected

and hard to replicate. If a product is not patentable and in the public domain, the company does *not* need you, they can make it themselves.

- **Has an advantage over existing products** – They do not want a "me-too" product. Your product should have a clear advantage over existing products.
- **Has received positive market tests** – It's best if you can show positive market test results from concept surveys, interviews, focus groups, and test sales.
- **Is ready to manufacture** – They do not want a product that's still in the idea stage. The best scenario is that the product is ready to manufacture.
- **Synergy** – Companies want a product that's related to their expertise in manufacturing, marketing, and sales. For example, a company that sells clothing is not going to be interested in licensing power tools.
- **Safety** – Companies are concerned about product liability lawsuits. Your product must be clearly safe to use. It also helps if your product is environmentally friendly.

The criteria for company acceptance are not unreasonable. If you were to self-market your product idea, you'd want the same for yourself.

Where to Find Companies to License Your Idea

There are many companies that might be interested in licensing your product. The trick is finding them. The Internet and local libraries provide good resources for finding company information.

Search for companies that produce or market products similar to yours. Use an Internet search engine and enter ["your product type" and "manufacturer"] as keywords. For example, if your product idea is a new communications device, enter ["communications equipment" and "manufacturer"] as keywords. Review the search results for company names. Go to each company's website to see what they do. Many websites have an "About" page describing the products and services they offer. Some will say they are in the business of licensing products. If they make no mention of licensing, send an email or call to find out if they license products. If they do, ask about their process.

The following Internet resources can help you locate companies that license products. The Internet changes often, so these websites may change. There are many free search services, so there's no need to pay for your search.

General Search Engines
- www.yahoo.com
- www.google.com
- www.altavista.com

Business Directories
- www.business.com
- www.thomasregister.com
- www.hoovers.com

Trade Magazines with Company Directories
- www.tradepub.com
- www.usubscribe.com
- www.newsdirectory.com

Trade Shows with Company Directories
- www.tradeshowweek.com
- www.tsnn.com
- www.yankeeinventionexpo.org
- www.internettradeshowslist.com
- www.globalsources.com

Write a Licensing Proposal

Companies will want to know more about you and your product idea. A Licensing Proposal is a formal statement you need to write that describes how great your product idea is, the advantages it has over existing products, who is going to buy it, how it will profit the company, and your credentials. In some cases, the company you approach has a form to fill out on their website. If not, submit the licensing proposal on your letterhead. Again, check their guidelines.

After completing the market research outlined in upcoming chapters, come back and use the following template to create your licensing proposal.

Licensing Proposal

Product Name

Patent Number

Product Type
Name the product type or product category (e.g., medical device, children's game, or software utility):

Need
Describe the market need for your product idea:

Gap
Describe how the market need is not being fulfilled:

Description
Describe how your idea solves a problem or satisfies a need or want, and how your idea looks, feels, and functions:

Competition
Name products that are similar and compete in the same market space:

Advantages
Describe your product's advantages over the competition:

Customer
Describe the typical customer who would use your product (e.g., age, sex, and socio-economic status, education, occupation, and income):

(continue)

Benefits
Describe the benefits derived from using your product (e.g., enhances safety, provides entertainment, saves money, makes money, or saves time):

Market
Describe the size of the market and trends related to your product:

Financial
Calculate revenue, cost of goods, expenses, and profit potential:

Inventor Bio
Provide personal background information (e.g., credentials, business experience, and industry familiarity):

Elements of a License Agreement

So what is a Licensing Agreement? A Licensing Agreement is a contract between you and the company that wishes to license your invention. It has certain legal language to cover the business transaction and specific terms, including time period, location, exclusivity, and payment. When a company wants to license your invention, it will draft a Licensing Agreement. A Licensing Agreement generally includes the following:

- **Time period** – The period of time that a company may manufacture, distribute, and sell your product (e.g., one year, five years).
- **Location** – Regions of the world where the company may manufacture, distribute, and sell your product (e.g., only United States, only Canada, North America, the entire world).

- **Exclusivity** – The number of companies you choose to license your product. "Exclusive Rights" means that only one company may license your product within a specified location over the time period. Usually, if you give one company exclusive rights, there's a higher royalty payment than a non-exclusive agreement in which many companies have the right to license your product.
- **Payment** – Terms of payment are expressed usually in a percentage of sales or number of units. It's common that a royalty equals 2% to 10% of net sales. What are net sales? Typically, net sales are the revenue generated. For example, if royalty payments are 5% of net sales and net sales are $200,000 the first year, then your royalty payment the first year is $10,000. Or, if your idea is a process being used to make something else, royalty payments are made for each unit produced. For example, royalty payments are $.10 for each metal spring produced by your new high-speed spring fabricator. Overall, negotiate for an advance payment to cover future royalties. The advance payment is yours whether or not they make or sell the product. For example, you receive an advance payment of $30,000 to cover the royalty payments of the first 10,000 units.

You have the right to be compensated for your efforts. And not every business opportunity is a good opportunity. If you feel pressured and uncomfortable with a business deal, it's better to walk away and find another. If possible, contact other inventors to see what kind of deals they negotiated.

Let Someone Else License the Idea for You

Do you like selling, making presentations, and negotiating contracts? If you've answered "Yes," then contact companies directly. 've answered "No," then use an Agent.

An Agent, also referred to as a Product Rep, is a broker between you and companies looking for new ideas. The Agent has industry contacts and knows how to pitch an idea. The Agent searches for companies that manufacture products similar to yours. Then, an Agent makes a presentation to company representatives. If the company is interested, the Agent negotiates on your behalf. Agents are on your side and try to get you the most money possible since they are getting a percentage of the deal. Working with an Agent involves the following steps:

1. Searching for Agents (see the next section to find an Agent).
2. Discussing with an Agent how they work and which industries they target.
3. Both you and the Agent signing a non-disclosure agreement to cover confidential issues such as marketing strategies and financial arrangements.
4. Sending the Agent a Licensing Proposal.
5. If the Agent likes the proposal, discussing terms for working together.
6. The Agent produces an Agent's Representative Agreement that allows the Agent to find a deal and get compensated.
7. Sending the Agent a prototype to use for presentations.
8. The Agent searches for business opportunities.
9. The Agent negotiates on your behalf to get the best deal.
10. The company generates a License Agreement that you review and sign.
11. You and the company carry out the License Agreement terms.

Some points concerning working with Agents:

- The Agent's Representative Agreement covers the Agent's responsibilities, your responsibilities, payment terms (usually 25% to 40%), a disclaimer clause, and a termination clause.

- Discuss allowable expenses the Agent may charge. Most Agent expenses should be their burden as the cost of doing their business.
- The terms of working together should be detailed in the Agent's Representative Agreement.
- Only work with Agents who do not request up-front payment. The Agent's Representative Agreement should specify that the Agent only receives payment as a result of generating revenue for you.

Where to Find Agents to License Your Idea

So if using an Agent seems appealing, where do you find one? Here are some options:

- Use an Internet search engine with ["your product type" and "product representative"] as keywords. For example, using Google, enter ["product representative" and "screwdrivers"] as keywords.
- Call manufacturers in your industry and ask if they use Agents or can recommend one.
- Search industry trade show directories and look for Agents or Product Reps that are listed as speakers or exhibitors.
- Call other inventors and ask for Agent recommendations.

Sell Rather Than License

In addition to licensing, you may assign your invention. "Assignment" is the legal term for selling your invention. The licensing process outlined above is the same process for assignments.

While negotiating, the company may indicate they want to own your invention rather than license it. Keep in mind that once you sell the invention, you longer have any rights to the patent. When you sell your invention, you receive a one-time lump sum or periodic payments (e.g., monthly, quarterly).

If you have the choice between a lump sum and periodic payments, compare periodic payments to a safe investment such as a money market or Certificate of Deposit. If the lump sum invested pays more than periodic payments, then take the lump sum. Also, check the tax consequences related to your tax bracket.

Now that you have an understanding of licensing, continue reading the following chapters to learn about market research and how to evaluate your product idea.

Part Two
MARKETABILITY

That's an amazing invention, but who would ever want to use one of them?

President Rutherford Hayes
(Referring to the telephone invented by Alexander Graham Bell.)

Chapter 6
The Role of Product Marketing

There is only one valid definition of business purpose: to create a satisfied customer. It is the customer who determines what the business is. Marketing is the whole business seen from the point of view of its final result. That is, from the customer's point of view.

Peter Drucker

When I was a young engineer, I thought marketing involved only advertising and picking colors. I didn't think marketing was much of anything. Later, I learned how marketing played a key role in creating new products. Product marketing has three primary objectives:

- Understand customer problems, needs, and wants (Market Research and Analysis).
- Translate problems, needs, and wants into products that customers want to buy (Product Planning).
- Communicate product benefits to generate awareness, interest, and sales (Marketing Communications).

The aim of your product is to deliver value to the customer. In return, the customer rewards you with money. Product marketing activities improve your chance of success. Researching customer needs will help you determine what the customer values. Once you know what customers value, you can create a product to meet, if not exceed, their expectations.

Now that we've entered the Internet Age, how have these three objectives changed? Of course the Internet helps to facilitate these objectives. But, you'll still have to understand customer needs and wants. And you'll still have to translate those needs into a product or service that customers are willing to buy or use.

The Internet provides new research, communication, and distribution tools. We can research competitors and collect market data quickly online. Direct email and banner advertising are tools to generate awareness and interest. And online shopping speeds the distribution process. And yet, while the Internet is a great tool, it does not change all of the rules. You'll still need to perform market research and create a product that people want.

What Market Data Are You Looking For?

The first step of the market research process is to determine which segment of the market your product belongs. Segments include:

- Audio / Video
- Automotive
- Beauty / Makeup / Hair / Personal
- Books
- Business Supplies
- Computer hardware
- Computer software
- Diet and Nutrition
- Entertainment
- Games and Hobbies
- Health and Fitness
- Housewares / Small Kitchen Appliances
- Jewelry
- Personal Development
- Small Tools
- Sporting Equipment

Next, you'll need to know the needs and wants of potential customers, market trends, competitors, success factors, and pricing. You'll need market research to answer these questions:

- Who will buy my product?
- How many people will buy my product?
- Where do they shop?
- How much do they typically spend?
- How do I get their attention?
- Who is my competition and how do I surpass them?
- What is the size of the market and is it growing?
- What trends will reduce or boost sales?
- Are there any regulations that apply to my product?

Market Research Sources

The Internet is a great place to begin your market research. And there are many search engines and databases that provide free information. These are some of my favorite websites for market research:

- Google (www.google.com)
- Yahoo (www.yahoo.com)
- Business (www.business.com)
- Webster's Online (www.webdir.net)
- United States Census Bureau (www.census.gov)
- United States Patent and Trademark Office (www.uspto.gov)

Use keywords that include your product type, such as "toy robot" along with "market trends," "market size," or "competition." The search engine will present links to news and company pages. Read as much as you can to learn about market dynamics.

While there's a lot of free information available, there are also detailed market reports you may buy for hundreds or thousands of dollars. These reports identify markets by categories and segments, segment size, future trends, market drivers for success, and key players. They're available from market research companies such as Gartner (www.gartner.com), Forrester (www.forrester.com), and IDC (www.idc.com).

In addition, you can find a wealth of market research in professional journals. Although these cost anywhere from $50 to $200, many of these market research journals are free at a public or university library. Look in the library's business, social science, or reference sections. Be prepared to read them on site because they cannot be checked out. The following are some of my favorite books for market research:

- **Industry Surveys** (Standard & Poor's) commentary of industry drivers, trends, and key businesses
- **Industry Handbook** (Dun & Bradstreet) commentary of industry drivers and trends
- **Industry Norms & Key Business Ratios** (Dun & Bradstreet) industry ratios of assets, liabilities, sales, and profit
- **US Market Trends & Forecasts** (Gale Group) market segments, market value, market share, and growth rate
- **Market Share Reporter** (Gale Group) market segments, market value, and market share
- **US Industry & Trade Outlook** (McGraw-Hill) detailed commentary of market segments

In addition, the library is likely to have free computer database search tools such as InfoTrac, ProQuest, New York Times Archive, or ABI/Inform. These databases will allow you to search through a wide variety of newspapers, professional publications, academic journals, and trade magazines.

Tip: Many public libraries provide vast amounts of information over the Internet. You may even be able to access database services from your home computer for free through your public library. Login with your library card number and a personal identification number (generally the last four digits of your telephone number) to gain access to dozens of normally costly databases. For example, the San Diego California Public Library website (sdplweb.sannet.gov) provides access to its library catalog as well as many databases for free.

How Much Market Research Is Needed?

Think of market research, analysis, and product planning as a form of risk reduction. In general, the more complex, costly, and time-consuming your product is to design and develop, the more up-front marketing activities are needed. If there's a large sum of money on the line, you'll want to eliminate as many risks as possible. For example, if your product requires a new integrated circuit designed by a team of engineers with a development cost of $2 million, you'll want to investigate the product's chance of success thoroughly.

On the other hand, if your prototype costs $5 to build, then go ahead and make a dozen for a market trial. Go to a swap meet or local event, rent a table, and see what kind of response you get. Or, put a small ad in the newspaper or magazine to see how many calls you receive.

Chapter 7
At What Stage Is Your Idea?

*A common mistake that people make when trying to design
something completely foolproof is to underestimate the
ingenuity of complete fools.*

Douglas Adams

If you have a new idea, or are currently developing a product or
service, take a minute to complete the following idea assessment
exercise. This exercise will reveal how much you've already
thought about your product idea.

A product involves much more than just the product itself.
Imagine you were opening a restaurant from scratch. What kind of
food are you personally good at preparing? Is the menu upscale,
medium-priced, or fast food? Is there a dance floor or a buffet
table? Will you need a big parking lot, or will customers arrive
by public transportation? Will people pay by credit card or cash?
Will you need to raise money for construction? How will you
promote the business? How will you generate repeat business?

Idea Assessment

The Idea Assessment on the next page asks you questions about
development, marketing, sales, and finance. Take a moment now
to complete as many as you can. Answer each question by cir-
cling "**Yes**" or "**No**." If you are not sure or don't have the information, circle the "**?**" question mark. Note that some of the
questions will ask what "you" have uncovered in a certain
situation. The term "you" refers to you as a sole proprietor, or
your team of co-workers, consultants, partners, or resources you
have or intend to obtain. I want you to succeed, so good luck!

Idea Assessment Questions

1.	Does your idea solve a particular problem, pain, need, or want?	Yes	No	?
2.	Does your idea have a particular advantage over existing products or similar methods?	Yes	No	?
3.	Have you received favorable feedback on your product idea?	Yes	No	?
4.	Have you identified the key features and benefits needed for your product idea?	Yes	No	?
5.	Have you identified the end-user of your product idea?	Yes	No	?
6.	Have you selected a target market?	Yes	No	?
7.	Do you know the size of the target market?	Yes	No	?
8.	Is the market for your idea growing?	Yes	No	?
9.	Do you know who your major competitors are?	Yes	No	?
10.	Do you know how you'll distribute and sell your product?	Yes	No	?
11.	Have you concluded that your idea will not infringe on any patents, trademarks, or copyrights?	Yes	No	?
12.	If necessary, will your product pass government regulations or third-party certification programs?	Yes	No	?
13.	Do you know the approximate cost to develop your idea into a product?	Yes	No	?

(continue)

14.	Do you know the approximate unit cost to manufacture your product?	Yes	No	?
15.	Do you know the approximate cost of business setup and administration?	Yes	No	?
16.	Do you know the approximate cost of marketing and selling your product?	Yes	No	?
17.	Do you know the price range that a customer is willing to pay for your product?	Yes	No	?
18.	Do you know how much time it will take to develop your idea into a sellable product?	Yes	No	?
19.	Do you have the technical know-how to design, develop, and build your product?	Yes	No	?
20.	Do you have the ability to market your product (advertising, promotion, etc.)?	Yes	No	?
21.	Do you have the ability to sell your product (direct, through a distributor, or license)?	Yes	No	?

How did you do? Did you score a lot of "Yes" answers? If not, help is just ahead. The purpose of this exercise was not to make you feel good or bad. It was to get you thinking about the entire product before you build it. The more you think through the issues up front, the better chance you have of creating a successful product.

These are the types of issues you'll need to think about before creating the blueprint and laying the foundation. Since you are the idea person, you'll need assistance in areas that are not your forte. Nobody knows *everything*, so you should absolutely seek help as necessary and needed.

Chapter 8
Simplified New Idea Process

Everyone is born a genius, but the process of living de-geniuses them.

R. Buckminster Fuller

As I've already mentioned in Chapter 2, "Your Roadmap to Success," the **Market-Step** process will take you from idea to launch, step-by-step. There are six key steps to self-market your product idea. To license your product idea, follow steps one through three before developing a licensing proposal. These key steps are:

1. **Flesh Out Your Idea** – Compare your idea to similar products in the market. Describe your idea in terms of customer benefits and features. Determine advantages over the competition. Evaluate profit potential.
2. **Test the Need** – Determine your target customer. Research the market for trends. Develop and use a concept survey to get feedback on your idea. Uncover customer problems, needs, and wants.
3. **Refine and Validate** – Create a prototype based on simple product requirements. Interview potential customers for detailed feedback. Make a decision to go forward, revise the idea, or scrap it all together.
4. **Plan It** – Perform in-depth development planning with customers in mind. Create detailed product requirements in terms of how it will look, perform, and be made. Determine positioning, pricing, distribution, marketing, sales strategies, and timeline.
5. **Develop It** – Create alpha and beta products for testing. Utilize a beta program for in-depth feedback on features

and functionality. Create marketing materials such as brochures, advertising, and websites.

6. **Launch It** – Complete the product and begin selling it. Issue a press release and launch full product promotion and sales. Evaluate your progress and make changes as needed.

Decision Paths

The **Market-Step** process contains Decision Paths at the end of each of the first three steps. A Decision Path is shown on the **Market-Step** process diagram labeled as Proceed, Revise, or Cancel. A Decision Path is a reality checkpoint to evaluate a step's results before moving on. If results are encouraging, you'll advance to the next step. If results are mixed, you might need to revise your idea. If results are very discouraging, revise the invention or cancel the project entirely to save yourself a lot of time and money.

How Long Does It Take?

How long will it take you to complete these six key steps to develop your product idea and make sales? That depends on the newness and complexity of your idea. For example, it took a few years for the costs of compact discs to come down to the point where average consumers could afford them. And then, it took some more years for people to give up their vinyl records and cassette tapes and to adopt CDs.

Simpler and less expensive products will usually gain acceptance more quickly in the market. A razor blade is a quick purchase decision. I'll spend a few dollars to try it. If I like it, I'll buy another, and tell others how much I liked it. On the other hand, million-dollar medical devices will go through a series of evaluations before customers will make a purchase.

The Market-Step™ Process Diagram

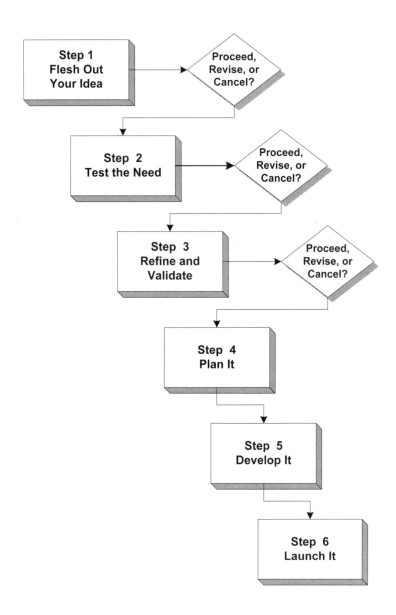

Time frame also depends, in part, on distribution. If your product is a software utility that can be downloaded from a website, distribution happens quickly. If your software product is very complex and must be sold by a field sales force, then the process of creating awareness and relationships will take longer.

Cutting down on development time is always desirable, but should *not* be accomplished by skipping important steps. The **Market-Step** process is flexible and efficient. In some cases, tasks may be carried out simultaneously. For example, during the Development Step, while engineering is developing the product, marketing may be working on advertising and promotional activities. Details for performing each activity are provided in each **Market-Step** process chapter.

Product Evolution

Products evolve through a series of stages. First, the idea is fleshed out in terms of the functions, features, and benefits that customers want. Then, products evolve through the following stages:

1. Prototype
2. Alpha
3. Beta
4. Commercial Release

Prototypes are used during early market research and market tests. You'll convert your product idea into a prototype so that people can evaluate your product visually. The prototype is a general working model with basic product features.

The product rendition after the prototype is known as an "alpha" product. The alpha product has basic functionality and is able to perform rudimentary tasks. It doesn't yet have fancy features, materials, or colors. It's just the basic product, suitable for internal testing and learning the development process.

The next rendition is known as the "beta" product. The beta product has enough of the key features and functions to provide a reasonable customer experience. The object is to get valuable feedback from potential customers before final touches are added. With beta feedback in mind, you'll create the commercial product release – a fully functional, tested, and packaged product ready to launch and sell.

In the chapters ahead, you'll take an idea and create a prototype. Then, your prototype will go through the development stages to become a successful product.

Chapter 9
Step One – Flesh Out Your Idea

Before you build a better mousetrap, it helps to know if there are any mice out there.

Mortimer Zuckerman

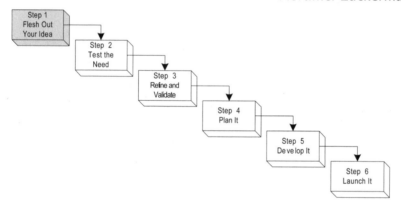

I'm excited for you! You have a great idea that you want to make into a successful product. Your first step in the **Market-Step** process is to flesh out your idea. We'll expand your idea in a systematic manner that will make your product come alive. We'll look at potential competitors, your product's benefits, its advantages, and then evaluate profit potential.

Are you going solo or with a team? In various parts of this book, I use the term "team" to mean the people assisting, developing, and marketing the product. The "team" may be just you, you and a spouse, you and a friend, you and consultants, a company team, or possibly partners.

Initially, you can go it alone to flesh out your idea and test the concept. But at some point, you'll need help from others. I'll assist you through each step of the process, and if you need extra help, I'll show you where to get it.

In Step One, you'll:

1. Describe your idea
2. Look for similar products
3. Uncover the benefits
4. Create competitive advantages
5. Determine a profit potential

What's Your Moneymaking Idea?

Our goal is to turn your idea into a winning product. Ideas come from a variety of sources as mentioned in Chapter 1. The first activity I want you to complete involves describing your idea. Use the Idea Description template to write down your thoughts. Don't worry about answering the exercise questions perfectly. The goal here is learning by doing. Either fill in the templates in this book, create your own templates, or download templates from my website (www.MattYubas.com).

Idea Description
What is the name or title of your idea?
What is your idea?
How does it work?
How did you come up with the idea?
What problem does it solve, or need or want does it fulfill?

Step One – Flesh Out Your Idea Flowchart

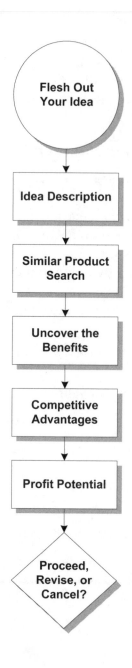

Find Similar Products

Are there any existing products that are similar to your invention? You need to know this up front. If you have an idea for a new robotic toy and there are 20 brands already out there, you'll have a difficult time selling yours unless it offers something special.

Suppose your idea is similar but has a new twist, then what? You'll need to investigate whether the new twist is enough to get people interested. I'll show you how to do that in the next chapter. For now, you'll need to complete a preliminary search for similar products. There may be products that are somewhat similar or very similar. We'll use this information later to determine your product's advantages, pricing, and positioning.

Remember, you'll want to make sure that if a similar product already exists, your invention must offer some advantage. Do not underestimate products that are technically inferior to yours. They might solve a particular problem that people want. In addition, keep track of products that your idea will replace. For example, if you had developed the first CD player, you would have evaluated cassette and record players to understand what advantages were needed to change habits.

Similar Products			
Company	Product	Price	Benefits and Features
Tin Robots	Gort Robot	$29.95	Wind up, walks, collectible box
Brainizord	Climb@tron	$15.99	Scales any smooth, non-porous vertical surface, bump-and-go auto-reverse action

The best place to start searching for competitors is on the Internet. Currently, my favorite Internet search engine is Google (www.google.com). You might also search for competitors using Business.com (www.business.com). In addition, my website (www.MattYubas.com) has many links to help you.

Start with some simple search terms, for example, "robot toy product" and see what you get. Click on the search results for products that look similar. Keep track of product names, company names, selling prices, benefits, and features. For more details, see "Investigate Your Competition" in Appendix A.

Similar Products			
Search for products similar to your idea and log them here.			
Company	Product	Price	Benefits and Features

Uncover the Benefits

What are the benefits and features of your idea? What problems does it solve? Which needs and wants will it satisfy? People buy based on benefits. Benefits have a powerful emotional appeal. Your product's benefits, not its features, will boost sales.

You might say, "Wait a minute! When I buy a car, I want a V8 engine, and that's a feature." Let's look a little closer at your want. Why do you want a V8 engine? You may need a car that will get up to speed quickly. You may need a car that's able to pull a heavy load, such as a boat. And you may like having power when you need it. So, in fact, the benefits you want are quickness, power, and peace of mind. You believe that V8 engines provide all these benefits. At least that's the message we get from the car manufacturers. But, there are probably cars with a V6 engine that will satisfy your needs just as well, cost less, and get better gas mileage. The point is to look at your product from a benefits point of view. If your invention does not provide any benefits, it will be difficult to sell. But, don't give up. You'll learn to transform product features and functions into benefits.

Benefits are different for business products versus consumer products. Businesses seek to remedy problems mainly related to revenue and efficiencies. Business benefits revolve around the bottom line – money. Your product will be an easy sell to businesses if it can generate higher revenue or save money. Business benefits sought are:

- **Higher Revenue and Higher Margins** – Businesses must generate revenue to survive. They'll invest in marketing campaigns, websites, and sales training programs.
- **Lower Costs and Higher Efficiency** – Businesses need to cut costs and increase efficiency to produce profits. Examples of products they'll invest in include automated equipment, computer software, and energy-efficient systems.
- **Higher Customer Retention** – Keeping a customer happy who buys more products is easier than trying to acquire new customers. Examples of products they'll invest in include customer relationship software, survey programs, and gifts.

Consumers seek products to remedy problems and satisfy needs and wants. Consumer benefits deal with personal motivators that are emotionally driven. Motivators include money, love, safety, recognition, acceptance, pleasure, and pain.

For example, what are the benefits and features of a new solar-powered flashlight? From the consumer's point of view, a solar flashlight provides safety, saves money, and saves time. The benefits and features are:

Benefits and Features	
Benefits (For Consumer)	Features
☑ Health and Safety	A solar rechargeable internal battery provides a constant light source that is longer than a standard flashlight.
☑ Save Money	With a solar rechargeable internal battery, there's no need to buy additional batteries.
☑ Save Time	With a solar rechargeable internal battery, there's no need to spend time shopping for batteries.

Benefits that consumers seek include:

- **Make Money** – We seek to make money to provide for basic survival, to gain love and recognition, and to use for pleasure. We work hard, educate ourselves, join clubs, and take on entrepreneurial adventures.
- **Save Money** – We like to save money so we have more of what money can do for us. We buy insulation for our homes to lower energy costs, buy fluorescent bulbs instead of incandescent, buy fuel-efficient cars, and cook our own meals instead of eating out at restaurants.
- **Save Time** – Time is our most precious commodity. Some people trade off between time and money. It may be quicker to fly 300 miles, but it's more expensive than driving. Time moves on, so we try to make the most of it. We buy organizers, dishwashers instead of dish drying racks, and send email instead of calling.
- **Safety, Health, Peace of Mind** – We want to stay healthy, so we enroll in fitness programs, get a physical, follow diet programs, and buy vitamins. And for safety,

we outfit our homes, cars, and offices with alarm
systems, take self-defense classes, and some buy guns.
- **Recognition and Acceptance** – We like feeling special
  and accepted. We join clubs, strive to win awards, and
  seek prestige in the things we buy.
- **Pleasure and Comfort** – Of course, we're motivated by
  pleasure. Why else would we eat ice cream and
  chocolate? We seek simple escapes like eating sweets, or
  more elaborate ones like taking a vacation to reduce
  stress.

By uncovering the benefits in your product, you can develop
marketing programs that appeal to your customers. What are
the benefits of your product idea? Check off the benefits and list
the associated features.

Benefits and Features	
Benefits (For Business)	Features
❑ Lower Costs	
❑ Higher Revenue	
❑ Higher Customer Retention	
Benefits (For Consumer)	Features
❑ Health and Safety	
❑ Make Money	
❑ Save Money	
❑ Save Time	
❑ Recognition / Acceptance	
❑ Pleasure	

Advantages Beat the Competition

The next step is to determine what advantages your product idea has over the competition. Think in terms of benefits. Let's use the solar-powered flashlight example. If it's the only one of its kind, it will have many advantages over battery-powered models. It will save money and time, and also provide peace of mind by lasting longer. If there are other solar-powered flashlights on the market, then the advantages are different because they all save time and money by not requiring batteries. Competitive advantages might be a waterproof or unbreakable aluminum case, or that it's less expensive than other models.

Product Advantages
What advantages does your product idea offer compared to the competition or similar products?

❑ Easier to use   ❑ Makes more money
❑ Faster   ❑ Saves more money
❑ More fun   ❑ Less expensive
❑ More efficient   ❑ Provides more safety
❑ Longer lasting   ❑ Provides more pleasure
❑ Saves more time   ❑ Other (explain):
❑ More stylish

I suggest that your product have at least two or more competitive advantages. If your product has only one market advantage and another product comes along with the same one, you no longer have an advantage.

Advantages are not limited to the product itself. For example, you might have access to technology that no one else has. Or, you have relationships with distributors that the competition does not. Or, you may obtain a patent that excludes others from creating a similar product.

What's the Profit Potential?

You want to know if your invention has a profit potential as soon as possible. Why spend a lot of time and money creating a product whose unit costs exceed the selling price? Or, why build a product whose expenses are so high that you'll never earn a profit? You'll need to develop a rough estimate of profit potential to see if product development makes sense. To determine profit potential, you'll need to estimate: Revenue Potential, Cost of Goods Sold, and Expenses.

Revenue Potential

Revenue is any cash received from product sales, licensing, or services. Two ingredients determine revenue potential: selling price and the number of product units you can sell. We have not determined an appropriate selling price yet, but let's look at prices of competitive products. For now, use the average or typical price the competition is charging as your selling price.

For a forecast of the number of units you can sell, try to get estimates of similar products. If any of the competitors are public companies, look at their annual reports. If the reports do not discuss how many units they sold, take the product revenue and divide it by the selling price, to provide the number of product units sold. If it's not a public company, ask store salespeople how many similar products they think are sold per year. Or, ask a trade association representative. In addition, you can buy market studies from research companies such as IDC, Gartner, or Forrester.

Once you have a forecast of total units sold in the market, come up with a percent estimate of the number of units you can sell based on the amount of marketing you might carry out.

For example, if a total of 10,000 solar flashlights are sold this year, then you can estimate you'll sell 5% of 10,000, which is 500. You'll sell 10% next year (1,000) and 20% (2,000) in year three.

Revenue Potential

First Year
1. What is the selling price? $ 20
2. How many can you sell?   1,000
Revenue: Multiply line 1 x line 2 $ 20,000

Second Year
1. What is the selling price? $ 20
2. How many can you sell?   5,000
Revenue: Multiply line 1 x line 2 $ 100,000

Third Year
1. What is the selling price? $ 20
2. How many can you sell?   20,000
Revenue: Multiply line 1 x line 2 $ 400,000

Revenue Potential

Determine the revenue potential for your product:

First Year
1. What is the selling price?
2. How many can you sell?
Revenue: Multiply line 1 x line 2 $

Second Year
1. What is the selling price?
2. How many can you sell?
Revenue: Multiply line 1 x line 2 $

Third Year
1. What is the selling price?
2. How many can you sell?
Revenue: Multiply line 1 x line 2 $

These are only estimates. If you're more conservative, use 1% the first year, then 5%, and then 10%. If you're more aggressive, then use 10% the first year, 20% the second, and 30% for the third year. Note that being more aggressive with sales forecasts indicates you'll spend more money on marketing and sales programs.

Cost of Goods Sold

Your product has costs that may include parts, labor, packaging, and sales commissions. It's more obvious with a tangible product such as a flashlight where each part has a cost, plus the cost to assemble, package, and distribute. A product such as software has small costs for each unit. Most of the costs associated with software are in development and marketing. Bill Gates once said that the first software package costs $50 million and the second, $2. The unit costs are a CD or DVD, duplication, documentation, packaging, and distribution. If your product is a software download, there are no unit costs, but only expenses of development and web support.

Cost of Goods Sold			
Each Part			Cost
Solar cell			2.10
Rechargeable battery			1.40
Switch			0.50
Case			0.50
Assembly			0.50
	Total Unit Cost		$ 5.00
Yearly Costs	Year 1	Year 2	Year 3
Units Sold	1,000	5,000	20,000
Total Unit Cost	$ 5.00	$ 4.00	$ 3.00
Cost of Goods	$ 5,000	$ 20,000	$ 60,000

Let's use the solar flashlight once more as an example for costs of goods. First, determine a list of parts and the cost of each part. Next, add these individual costs to get a total unit cost. Then, multiply the number of units sold by the total unit cost. Note how, in the second and third year, costs come down due to volume purchases or from using a less expensive supplier.

If you do not know the cost of each part, talk to an accountant who specializes in the industry related to your idea. Also, talk with an industry trade association in your field for industry averages of costs.

Cost of Goods Sold			
Determine the cost of goods sold for your product.			

Each Part			Cost
	Total Unit Cost		$

Yearly Costs	Year 1	Year 2	Year 3
Units Sold			
Total Unit Cost			
Cost of Goods	$	$	$

Product and Business Expenses

Expenses include all costs related to developing, marketing, and selling products, as well as administrative and startup costs. There are a variety of expenses associated with turning an idea into a product – startup and ongoing monthly expenses. The following are a list of possible expenses. I suggest you talk with an accountant or a trade association in your field for industry averages of expenses related to your product.

Expense Estimates

Determine the one-time startup and monthly expenses for your product idea.

	Year 1	Year 2	Year 3
One-time			
Accounting Fees			
Computer Hardware			
Computer Software			
Equipment			
Furniture			
Incorporation			
Legal Fees			
Market Research			
Product Certification			
Product Prototype			
Product Testing			
Packaging			
Promotions			
Telephones			
Miscellaneous			
Total One-time	$	$	$
Monthly			
Labor			
Office Rent			
Lease Payments			
Loan Payments			
Office Supplies			
Miscellaneous			
Total Monthly	$	$	$

Profit Potential

Now that you've determined revenue potential, costs of goods sold, and expenses, you can calculate profit potential. Note that net profit will be reduced by taxes. Please review the numbers in the following example.

In the first year, a thousand units were sold at $20 a piece, leading to $20,000 of revenue. Since each product costs $5, the product costs of goods from selling 1,000 units are $5,000. Therefore, gross profit is $15,000. When you subtract expenses of $25,000, the net profit in this case is a loss of $10,000. But don't worry; it's very common for losses to occur during the first year. Formulas for determining profit include:

- Revenue = Number of Units Sold x Selling Price
- Cost of Goods = Number of Units Sold x Unit Cost
- Gross Profit = Revenue - Cost of Goods Sold
- Expenses = One-time Expenses + Monthly Expenses
- Net Profit = Gross Profit - Expenses

Profit Potential			
Revenue	Year 1	Year 2	Year 3
Units Sold	1,000	5,000	20,000
Selling Price	$20	$20	$15
Total	$ 20,000	$100,000	$300,000
Cost of Goods	$(5,000)	$(20,000)	$(60,000)
Gross Profit	$ 15,000	$ 80,000	$240,000
Expenses			
One-time	$13,000	$1,000	$4,000
Monthly x 12	$12,000	$24,000	$36,000
	$(25,000)	$(25,000)	$(40,000)
Net Profit	$(10,000)	$ 55,000	$ 200,000

Profit Potential

Determine the profit potential for your product idea.

Revenue	Year 1	Year 2	Year 3
Units Sold			
Selling Price			
Total	$	$	$
Cost of Goods			
Gross Profit	$	$	$
Expenses			
One-time			
Monthly x 12			
	$	$	$
Net Profit	$	$	$

Profit Potential

Try different scenarios of either units sold, selling price, cost of goods, or expenses to determine profit potential.

Revenue	Year 1	Year 2	Year 3
Units Sold			
Selling Price			
Total	$	$	$
Cost of Goods			
Gross Profit	$	$	$
Expenses			
One-time			
Monthly x 12			
	$	$	$
Net Profit	$	$	$

Decision Path One

The Decision Path is a quick review to see if your idea makes sense so far. For each of the following questions, circle "**Yes**" or "**No**." If you're not sure of the answer, circle the "**?**" question mark.

Decision Path One			
1. Does your product idea solve a particular problem, pain, need, or want?	Yes	No	?
2. Does your product idea offer benefits to either a business or consumer?	Yes	No	?
3. Do you know who your competitors are?	Yes	No	?
4. Does your product idea have advantages over similar products?	Yes	No	?
5. Does your product idea make sense financially?	Yes	No	?

If you answered "Yes" to these questions, you're on the right track and may move on to Step Two. If you had any "No" responses, revise your invention to satisfy potential deficiencies and then continue. If you answered "?" to a few of these questions and are waiting for more information, you may move to the next step knowing that the answers may or may not ultimately be favorable.

You have done an excellent job to get to this point! Congratulate yourself and move on to Step Two.

Chapter 10
How Your Customer Thinks

There is only one boss. The customer. And he can fire everybody in the company from the chairman on down, simply by spending his money somewhere else.

Sam Walton

Knowing your customer provides insight about how to make your product idea more attractive and sellable. There are four points to consider:

- Customers buy when they want to solve a problem or when they want to satisfy a need or want
- Customers do not buy alone, they're influenced by other people
- Customers buy according to their personality
- Customers follow a process before they buy

Customer Problems, Needs, and Wants

When you go to a doctor, what happens? After reading countless magazines, you're called into the examination room. A nurse asks some questions and takes some vitals. Then the doctor comes in, looks at your chart, and asks questions. Where does it hurt? How long have you had that? Does it hurt when you move? The doctor is attempting to isolate the problem to offer a solution. What if your doctor just handed out pills without asking any questions? The point is that you need to understand the customer's problem before offering a solution (your product). Typically, problems center on a lack of money, love, health, esteem, recognition, and satisfaction.

The Many Faces of a Customer

Let's uncover how a customer goes about making a purchase. There's usually more than one person involved in the buying decision process. For example, a child's toy may have as many as four people involved. The child's friend (first person) starts the process by convincing the child (second person) that he needs a certain toy. The child will initiate the buying process by telling the parent (third person) he needs a certain toy. The child might beg and cry to get what he wants. The child is the user of the toy, but the parent is the buyer, and another adult (fourth person) may be involved in making the final decision. In the end, the child, the child's friend, and the parents are all involved in the buying process.

How does the buying process affect you, the product developer? The buying process implies that your product design and marketing communications needs to appeal to various people. For example, to appeal to the child and child's friend, the toy may need to be red and make a lot of noise. To appeal to the parents, it must be safe, easy to assemble, and reasonably priced.

Who is involved in the buying process for a business? Whereas consumers mostly involve friends, family, and product reviews. Business customers act differently. Each business has a chain-of-command for evaluating purchases. Your product has to appeal to each person and department involved. For example, a software product must appeal to the Information Technology Manager based on technical merit. The Purchasing Manager must like the warranty and terms. And, the Chief Technology Officer must like the return on investment.

Here are roles generally played by different people in the buying process:

- **Initiator** – This is the person(s) who gets things started. This may be the neighbor with the new car, a friend who describes a new bicycle, or an analyst who discovers a flaw in a business process.

- **Influencer** – This is the person(s) who advocates making the purchase. It may be a crying child, it could be a parent, or a boss.
- **Decider** – This is the person(s) who makes the final purchase decision. This could be the Initiator, the purchasing department, or a spouse.
- **Buyer** – This is the person who hands over the cash, check, or credit card. The Buyer and Decider might be the same person or different people.
- **User** – The actual user(s) of the product.

I've Got to Have It First

Do you have a friend or family member who is always first to have the latest gadget? I have an uncle who is that way. I remember he had the first digital watch. He paid hundreds of dollars for it back in the 1970s. It's only function was to tell the time with its four bright red numbers. Today, a $10 Casio watch performs a series of magic tricks in comparison to that first digital watch.

Another example is the microwave oven. Microwave ovens provide time savings and convenient cooking. People who liked the latest gadgets bought them right away. They accepted the microwave's benefits and trusted the safety. Risk-adverse people waited years. Either they worried about the possible effects of radiation, could not justify the price, or saw no reason to switch their cooking method. Most of us occupy the middle ground. We don't buy right away and want to hear reports or experience of others before making a decision.

The authors of *Crossing the Chasm* (Geoffrey Moore) and *The Diffusion of Innovation* (Everett Rogers) explain how different types of people have different comfort levels for trying and buying new products. Studies have proven this concept especially as it pertains to technology-based products. When a new product becomes available, the different lengths of time people wait to make a purchase is based on their personality type. This is important for product developers to know. When a new product is introduced, it's first purchased by an Innovator, then an Early Adopter, Early Majority, Late Majority, and last but not least, the Laggards.

- **Innovator** – They love new gadgets for the sake of technology and style rather than their role in solving particular problems. They're visionaries, risk-takers, and global thinkers. They're roughly 3% of your market.
- **Early Adopter** – They're risk-takers and role models who test the waters ahead of most people in their peer group. They try an innovation and offer opinions on their experience. They're roughly 12% of your market.
- **Early Majority** – They're practical and somewhat conservative. They want value and require proof that your product will do the job. They're roughly 35% of your market.
- **Late Majority** – Being cautious and skeptical, they weigh pros and cons, and still sometimes need peer pressure to finally make a purchase decision. They're roughly 35% of your market.
- **Laggards** – Laggards are late to change and sometimes suspicious. They take a long time to make a decision. They're roughly 10% of your market.

There's nothing wrong with being any of these personality type categories. In fact, we may be an Early Adopter in some instances and a Late Majority in others. It depends on our comfort level for a particular product type.

How will these different personality types affect you as a seller? There's good news and bad news. The good news is that there are always Innovators, those people who will buy anything if the product is innovative and confers some prestige to its owner. They've got to have your product and will pay almost anything to get it. The bad news is that this can give you false hope. When Innovators snap up your product, you think you'll become a millionaire in no time. The truth is that the rest of the market does not buy like the Innovators. The rest of the market is more skeptical. They need to see real results, they want form and function, and they want reasonable prices

The solution to selling to different personality types is two-fold. When you first market your product, the Innovator marketing message focuses on innovation, uniqueness, and the exclusivity of owning your product. You then need to persuade Innovators and Early Adopters to evangelize for you. Get their testimonials, get them to speak for you, and ask them to spread the word. Since they're role models, others will take their advice and buy your product.

Secondly, take the early revenue and plow it back into the business. To attract the rest of the market, the Early Majority types and others, you'll need to deliver benefit-oriented marketing messages. Advertising and promotion creates awareness (hype or buzz), overcomes risk-adverse behaviors, generates interest, and stimulates product purchase.

Know the Customer's Buying Process

We all go through a buying process. The only thing that varies is the time it takes to make a purchase decision. For example, buying a car is more involved and takes longer than buying an inexpensive product such as chewing gum. This is important to know as a product developer. First, we recognize a problem, need, or want. Then we search for information and sift through the facts. We evaluate the alternatives and make a purchase. If we are looking for chewing gum, the process can take 30 seconds. A car purchase can take up to 30 days. The following outlines the general buying process:

1. **Problem Recognition** – We realize we need to make a change. For example, you discover the soles of your shoes are worn out after you just stepped in a puddle (problem). Or, your neighbor just purchased a new car and you feel like keeping up with the Jones' (want).
2. **Information Search** – Now that we've realized a problem, are in pain, or have a need or want, it's time to

search for solutions. Some people read consumer magazines and gather information over the Internet. Some people go to a retail store, look at a few products, and ask a salesperson for help.

3. **Evaluation of Alternatives** – In our mind, we hold beliefs about how a product should function, what the product should look like, and the benefits it should deliver. We have some beliefs based on brand recognition from the bombardment of marketing. From these perceptions and others such as price, packaging, and availability, we narrow our selection to a few choices.

4. **Purchase Decision** – Product selection may take minutes, hours, or even months. Just before making a decision, the customer is often influenced by comments and suggestions of Influencers and Decision Makers. This could be from a friend, family member, salesperson, or comments read on the Internet. In addition, there could be last-minute decisions after weighing price versus benefits.

5. **Post-purchase** – Once the purchase is made, relief follows because a solution has been found. But sometimes buyer's remorse sets in and we wonder if we made the right decision.

How does the customer buying process affect us as product developers? We need to understand the buying process for our type of product. In the problem recognition phase, we need to know what types of problems people have that our product seeks to solve. We need to know who customers listen to when gathering information. Do they read *Consumer Reports*, follow the advice of a famous athlete, or listen only to Mom?

We need to make sure that customers are aware of our product when they begin their search so we are in the running for evaluation. Advertising and promotion accomplish this. And when they evaluate us, we have already anticipated, through market research, their problems, pains, needs, and wants. Therefore, customers will view our product as a viable solution.

We also know that word-of-mouth advertising is effective, so we make sure to offer a quality product and excellent service. Finally, we solve post-purchase buyer's remorse by including a thank-you letter with the product, sending a thank-you letter, or making a follow-up telephone call congratulating them for making the right purchase decision, and offering product support if the need arises.

During the entire development process, you'll need to think about your product from the customer's point of view. And the best way to get information about your customers is to interact with them. I'll lead you through the process of surveying and interviewing customers to uncover their needs and wants.

Chapter 11
Step Two – Test the Need

One of the most common marketing mistakes is for the owner to assume that his or her tastes, together with the tastes of immediate family, are universal.

Howard Upton

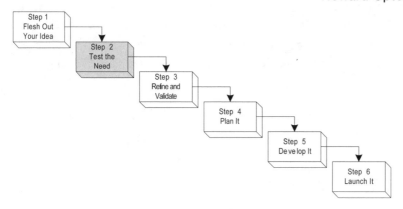

During the second step of the **Market-Step** process, you'll test the need. In this step, we'll identify potential end-users and have them review your product idea. I emphasize the term *end-users* rather than buyers. If your buyer is a retail store, then the end-user would be the retailer's customer. You might convince a store to carry your product, but if the end-users are dissatisfied and return your product, the retailer will no longer want to carry it. So, you'll want to make sure that end-users will be happy with your product.

Using the methods in Step Two, you'll get a reasonable understanding of the market need for your idea. First, you'll identify your potential customer. It's important to know the characteristics of your customers and the market groups to which they belong. Then, you'll need to survey potential customers to determine how receptive they are to your product idea. This market research method lets us easily get a feel of how well the product will succeed before creating a prototype. In addition, after you get a number of positive responses, you can show the results to investors, retailers, and companies that are interested in licensing.

Before you discuss or demonstrate your invention, it's a good idea to get a non-disclosure agreement (NDA) signed by the people evaluating your idea. An NDA does not provide 100% protection, but sends a signal to others that you intend to protect your rights if need be. Have an attorney create an NDA for you. To save money, you can find a generic NDA form on the Internet using the search terms "NDA" and "form." You can then tailor this form by adding wording that describes your product. A generic form offers less protection, but it's better than no protection at all.

In Step Two, you'll:

1. Identify your potential future customers
2. Survey future customers to get feedback
3. Get more details with interviews

Who Is Your Future Customer?

You'll need to identify who'll be interested in your product. The following methods will help you identify future customers:

- Brainstorm to create a list of potential groups of people (or types of companies) that could benefit most from your product.
- Talk to retailers and distributors to understand who buys similar or competitive products.
- View websites and packaging of similar and competitive products and notice the type of customers they target.

Step Two – Concept Evaluation Flowchart

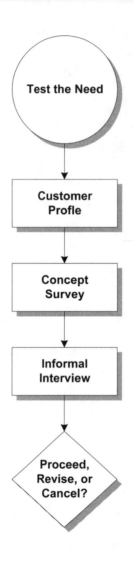

To identify your target customer, start with the competitive products you researched in Step One. Who are the buyers for those products? Customers are usually identified in marketing literature, on the website, or on their product box. For example, a toy's packaging might indicate that it's for children ages six to ten. Or, a brochure for a computer product might note that the product is intended for Information Technology Managers, road warriors, and home office users.

If similar products do not provide a customer profile, then brainstorm possible users. For example, if your idea is a new type of screwdriver, then think about who currently uses them. You might conclude that screwdrivers are primarily used by Auto Mechanics, Carpenters, and Homeowners over the age of 65. This is a good start.

Also, ask yourself "What types of people (or companies) have the greatest need or want for my product?" If your product benefit is a time saver, then who will save the most time by using your product? If your product benefit is a money saver, then who will save the most money by using your product? If your product benefit is entertainment, then who will most appreciate the fun and pleasure delivered by your product?

Customer Groups
Name at least three groups who might benefit from using your product:
Group 1: _____
Group 2: _____
Group 3: _____

If potential groups of end-users of your product idea are not obvious, use the Internet for research. For example, use a search engine such as Google (www.google.com) and enter keywords ["screwdriver" and "customers"] or ["screwdriver" and "market segment"]. Search results might include various articles, press releases, and product information. Review the information, looking for different types of people and businesses mentioned as users. They're your potential future customers.

Once you've identified potential customer segments, you'll need to study their characteristics. For example, a new screwdriver might be best used by Auto Mechanics (Group name), who are predominately male (sex), between 18–45 (age), in all parts of the country (business location), and in a retail service business (type). This information will help you create a customer profile for later use.

Sample Customer Profile			
	1	2	3
Group name:	Auto Mechanics	Carpenters	Homeowners 65+
Personal			
Age range:	18–45	18–45	65–75
Education:	high school	high school	high school
Family size:			
Income:			
Location:	all	all	all
Nationality:			
Occupation:	auto mech.	carpenters	all
Race:			
Religion:			
Sex:	M	M	all
Social class:			
Business			
Industry:	auto repair	new homes	
Location:	all	all	
Size:	small	all	
Type: *			
* Manufacturer, Distributor, Retailer, Government			

Another approach to uncover potential customer involves talking with retailers and distributors who sell products similar to yours. Talk to sales people, managers, and purchasing people. For example, go into a Home Depot and speak to workers in the hardware department. Let them know you're working on a new type of screwdriver. Then, mention that you're curious to know who buys similar types of screwdrivers. The people they mention are your potential customers.

Customer Profile		
Enter three groups of potential customers and their demographics.		
1	2	3
Group name: _____	_____	_____
Personal _____	_____	_____
Age range: _____	_____	_____
Education: _____	_____	_____
Family size: _____	_____	_____
Income: _____	_____	_____
Location: _____	_____	_____
Nationality: _____	_____	_____
Occupation: _____	_____	_____
Race: _____	_____	_____
Religion: _____	_____	_____
Sex: _____	_____	_____
Social class: _____	_____	_____
Business _____	_____	_____
Industry: _____	_____	_____
Location: _____	_____	_____
Size: _____	_____	_____
Type: * _____	_____	_____
* Manufacturer, Distributor, Retailer, Government		

If your product will be new to the world, search for people who already use a product that you're hoping to replace. For example, if you had developed the DVD player, you might have talked with people who owned a CD, LaserDisc player, or VCR. Or, if you'd developed the first word processor, you might have talked with people who used a typewriter.

Who are potential groups of people or businesses that can benefit most from your product idea? Please review the sample customer profile and then enter three groups of potential customers and their characteristics. You'll want to be as detailed and specific as possible. For more details, see "Select Your Target Market" in Appendix B.

Create a Concept Survey

Before spending money on a prototype, get feedback on your idea by launching a concept survey. A concept survey is a questionnaire that lists problems and describes how your idea solves them. It uncovers issues such as product need, estimate of perceived benefits, willingness to buy, and amount willing to spend. In addition, the concept survey may uncover new uses, new features, and new benefits.

In general, people like to help and contribute to something new. Let them know upfront that you're not selling them anything, but that you're researching a new product idea. To find people to take your survey, look for user or trade groups who meet to discuss interests that relate to your product.

I look for meeting announcements in local newspapers or on websites. Then, I call ahead or show up at the meeting early. I ask the leader if the group could participate in a five-minute survey. I emphasize that I'm not trying to sell anything. I have a new product idea and am interested in feedback. I hand out the surveys, collect them in five minutes, and thank them for their time. Other options to find people to take your survey include swap meets, shopping malls, trade shows, and schools.

Sample Survey – Self-correcting Household Clock

This is a brief survey to get your feedback on a new product idea. Please read the following description and then answer the questions.

It's a common problem that the clocks in our home each have different times displayed. Each clock seems to run at a different pace. As a result, we can miss appointments or create confusion.

A new product is being developed to correct this problem. This new household clock has a built-in mechanism to display the correct time within one second. These new clocks pick up the signals sent by the ultra-precise U.S. Atomic Clock. As a result, every clock in your home will display the correct time, and you'll never have to adjust your clocks again.

Please answer the following questions.

1. Of the clock problems stated above, how much does this affect you?
❑ Always ❑ Most of the time ❑ Sometimes ❑ Rarely ❑ Never

2. How well do you believe this new product will solve the problem?
❑ Excellent ❑ Very Good ❑ Somewhat ❑ Poor ❑ Not at all

3. If this product was available, and the price was reasonable, would you likely purchase a product like this for yourself or as a gift (you're not under any obligation to do so)?
❑ Definitely ❑ Very likely ❑ Somewhat ❑ Unlikely ❑ Not at all

4. Where would you normally purchase a product like this?

Your comments or suggestions to improve this product idea:

Thank you for your time!

Purpose

Problem

Diagram

Solution

Survey Questions

Concept Survey

Use this template as a guide to create your concept survey.

Title
Provide a title that describes your idea.

Purpose
Describe the purpose of this survey.

Problem
Describe the problem that a customer typically encounters.

Diagram
Provide a picture, drawing, or screen grab of something that is familiar relative to your idea. Use an existing product that people can readily identify rather than a representation of your product idea.

Solution
Write a short paragraph of how your invention solves the problem.

Survey Questions
Ask three to four questions to determine how they liked your solution.

Comments
Ask for comments and suggestions.

I suggest you collect data from a sample size of at least thirty people in each potential market segment. The higher the sample size the better.

To summarize results, count the total number of surveys and the number of positive surveys in each group. A positive response to a question is when people checked either the highest or second highest positive indicator on the scale (e.g., "Excellent" or

"Very Good"). Overall, at least 80% of the surveys should express a positive rating before you can assume that you'll likely have a successful product. The group with the highest rating is possibly your target market.

Concept Survey Results

Use this table to tabulate the results of your concept surveys.

Group 1 Name: _____
Number of concept surveys: _____
Number that received a positive rating: _____
Percent positive (positive / number surveys):   _____

Group 2 Name: _____
Number of concept surveys: _____
Number that received a positive rating: _____
Percent positive (positive / number surveys):   _____

Group 3 Name: _____
Number of concept surveys: _____
Number that received a positive rating: _____
Percent positive (positive / number surveys):   _____

Get More Details with Informal Interviews

Often, people who take a concept survey are interested in your product and want to know more. When someone seems interested in your idea, use that as a sign to ask a few more questions. Information you gather with informal interviews is used to add or refine product features and functionality.

Uncover what's important in performance, look, feel, or other characteristics related to your invention. Not only should you listen for features, but also for benefits. People want new ways to do things better. They want to look better, feel better, make money, and be more efficient to save time.

Compare to Similar Products

In addition to uncovering desired product characteristics, you'll want to find out how your new product idea provides a better solution than the competition. A good place to start is by asking questions to uncover what future customers might want, compared to what they are currently using.

Important Product Characteristics

From interviews, use the chart below to check off important criteria that interests your potential customers.

- ❑ Color
- ❑ Customer service
- ❑ Dependability
- ❑ Documentation
- ❑ Durability
- ❑ Ease of installation
- ❑ Ease of use
- ❑ Materials
- ❑ Packaging

- ❑ Place of purchase
- ❑ Sound
- ❑ Speed
- ❑ Style
- ❑ Value
- ❑ Visual appeal
- ❑ Warranty
- ❑ Other:

Find people who use a similar product to your invention and ask the following type of questions:

- If there were one thing that you wish (fill in name of a similar product they are using) could do better, what would it be?
- When using that product, is it (fill in a key product attribute – e.g., fast enough, easy to use, small enough, efficient, fun to use, cost effective, etc.)?
- When using that product, does it (fill in a key product failure – e.g., break down often, wear out, leak, crash often, produce the wrong results, act unreliably, etc.)?
- What features and benefits do you look for when choosing that type of product?

- What is most important to you: product quality, service, or price?
- What would it take for you to switch to a new product?

The answers to these questions will provide a foundation for establishing your product features and functions. In addition, they'll help shape your future marketing communications.

For example, potential markets for a new type of screwdriver might include Carpenters, Auto Mechanics, and Homeowners over the age of 65. For each market segment you'd ask the following questions:

- If there were one thing you wish your Philips screwdriver could do better, what would it be?
- When using a Philips screwdriver, is it easy and efficient to use?
- When using a Philips screwdriver, how often does it wear out?
- What features and benefits do you look for when choosing screwdrivers?
- What is most important to you: product quality, functionality, customer service, warranty, or price?
- What would it take for you to switch to a new screwdriver?

In this example, Carpenters were asked the above questions. As a result, most had no real issues with the screwdriver they were using. It worked just fine and they saw no need to switch.

Auto Mechanics, however, wished there was a better screwdriver. You then gather detailed descriptions of their problems, pain, needs, and wants. A hypothetical summary of what Auto Mechanics said about using a Philips screwdriver:

- Their hands fatigue easily and they have to take frequent breaks (problem).
- A reasonable percentage have developed carpal tunnel syndrome (pain).

- The screw-heads wear out quickly and they'd prefer a metal that does not erode (need).
- They'd like something with easily interchangeable screw heads (want).

Asking Homeowners over the age of 65 the same questions revealed that most had only a few problems because they only make minor repairs themselves. They call a contractor for major repairs.

In summary, interviews identified one market segment (Auto Mechanics) that had a strong need. This tells you there's probably a market for your invention.

Decision Path Two

The Decision Path is a quick review to see if your idea makes sense so far. For each of the following questions, circle "**Yes**" or "**No**." If you're not sure of the answer, circle the "**?**" question mark.

Decision Path Two			
1. Have you identified a group of potential customers for your idea?	Yes	No	?
2. Have you received favorable results from your Concept Survey (at least 80% of those surveyed gave top scores)?	Yes	No	?
3. Have you identified specific characteristics of your invention that are important to your potential customer?	Yes	No	?

If you answered "Yes" to all of these questions, you're on the right track. Compliment yourself and move on to Step Three. If not, revise your idea, and then follow the sequence outlined in this chapter to see if you generate a better response.

Chapter 12
Step Three – Refine and Validate

The whole of science is nothing more than a refinement of everyday thinking.

Albert Einstein

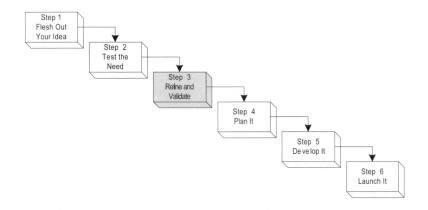

During the third step of the **Market-Step** process, you'll refine your idea into a prototype and have it validated by potential customers.

In general, people want to see physical representations of tangible products, or view sample screens of software products or websites. If your prototype is extremely complex to develop, you might be able to use diagrams or designs either on paper or as a software simulation. In either event, you'll want to create a way for someone to see and understand how your product will look and operate.

Step Three might require a few iterations during which you'd create a prototype, get feedback, modify the prototype, and then get more feedback. For example, if the first prototype doesn't receive a good response, you'll want to review the feedback and improve the prototype. And then see if you get positive evaluations the next time around.

In Step Three, you'll:

Turn your idea into a prototype
1. Uncover user scenarios
2. Create prototype requirements
3. Develop a prototype

Validate your prototype
4. Create an interview plan
5. Recruit people to interview
6. Conduct the interview
7. Summarize the feedback

If you're completing Step Three yourself, perform activities one through seven in consecutive order. If two or more people are involved, you can save time by working in tandem. A person or team can perform activities one through three, while the other works on activities four and five. Then, when a prototype is ready, complete activities six and seven together.

TURN YOUR IDEA INTO A PROTOTYPE

You'll want to get feedback on both the visual and functional aspects of your prototype. For example, a new cell phone would be evaluated for how it operates as well as its design appeal. Since the cell phone must function according to industry standards, it will have to be tested and certified by engineers. At the same time, the cell phone will need to have a look and feel that's accepted by the target market.

Step Three – Prototype Evaluation Flowchart

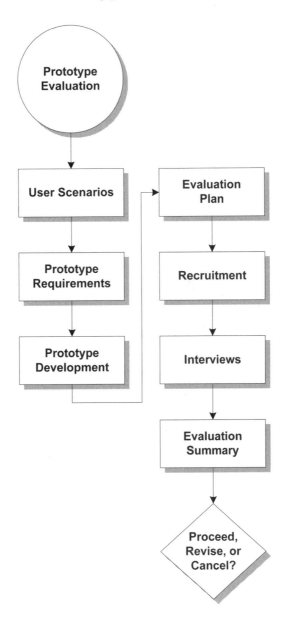

The key steps to creating a prototype involve:

- Stating your prototype goals
- Developing user scenarios
- Writing prototype requirements
- Sketching a design
- Searching for a designer (or designing it yourself)
- Searching for a prototype manufacturer

Prototype Goals
Select the goals for your prototype (✓): ❑ Determine if the idea functions as imagined ❑ Have users evaluate the look and feel ❑ Have users evaluate the functionality ❑ Get investors interested ❑ Get licensing companies interested ❑ Other:

User Scenarios

User Scenarios involve simply observing people using a product. You'll want your product to fit with the way someone would normally use your type of product. People are more likely to adopt a product that's simple and familiar. If it's too awkward to use, the customer will either return the product or not use it at all.

For example, a Microsoft Windows® software application menu structure typically includes File, Edit, Tools, and Help items. If your product has none of these, users may reject your product since it seems unfamiliar and thus unintuitive. Similarly, if most people are accustomed to CD players with power and play buttons on the left side, you'll want yours to use a similar arrangement. The exception would be if your product positioning is style rather than practicality. For example, Bang and Olufsen makes high-end stereo products and focuses on style as its key selling point.

To start, observe and interview people as they perform tasks with a product that's similar to your invention. This will give you insight on how people will want to use your product.

After observing and interviewing at least ten people, summarize the results. You might be surprised to learn that people will use your product differently than you expected or intended. These insights can often lead to new features, or possibly spin-off products and accessories.

User Scenarios

Use the following template to record your observations of people using a product that is similar to yours.

Install
What are the steps someone goes through to install or assemble your type of product when they first get it?

Turn on and Use
What are the steps someone goes through to turn on, start, or put on and then use your type of product?

Turn off
What are the steps someone goes through to turn off, put away, uninstall, or disassemble your type of product?

Tools
What tools are needed to install, assemble, use, uninstall, or disassemble your type of product?

These observations will help ensure that your product will be familiar enough to increase the probability of product acceptance. One good strategy involves designing your invention with a generally accepted look and feel of a known product, and then integrating your innovation to add value and uniqueness.

Prototype Requirements

A Prototype Requirements document describes how the prototype will function, how it will look and feel, what problems it will solve, and a general flow of how it will operate. It compliments drawings and diagrams. Creating a Prototype Requirements document is especially important if the prototype is complicated, or you plan to have it produced by someone else. A Prototype Requirements document describes features, quality guidelines, materials, performance, and durability. Sources of requirements come from:

- **Customer problems, needs, and wants** – Derived from surveys, interviews, and market trends.
- **Customer price sensitivity** – Derived from surveys and interviews to determine the quality of the parts used.
- **Competitive advantages** – Derived from competitive research to determine what features and functionality will overcome the competition.
- **Innovation** – Derived from your imagination.

I suggest creating a Prototype Requirements document with the following steps:

1. List each of the customer's problems, needs, and wants.
2. For each problem, need, and want, make lists of features and functions that provide solutions.
3. Modify and enhance features and functions based on your positioning, pricing, quality, style, and product life.
4. Prioritize the list based on saleable features and functions customers are willing buy.
5. Write the list of features and functions into the language of a requirements document.

6. Select the highest priority requirements that can be produced quickly and within budget.
7. Include drawings and pictures for clarification.

The language of a requirements document is in the form of, "The product shall have the ability to ..." or "The product must operate under the following conditions: ..." The requirements document must be clear and straightforward. Use bulleted or numbered lists and group similar parameters. For example, a cell phone's requirements might include:

- The prototype must be 3" long, 1" wide, and ½" thick.
- The prototype is made from clear solid plastic.
- The prototype must not break apart when dropped onto a solid floor from a height of three feet.

Using the customer's point of view is one key to product success. A requirements document will clarify the design and improve the quality of the prototype.

Prototype Development

Prototypes are made to evaluate physical products, electronic designs, and software applications or websites. There are a number of prototype methods for turning your idea into a visual or functional model. To begin you'll want to select a prototype method that's simple to build.

Prototypes commonly go through a number of iterations, so start with an inexpensive prototype for quick feedback to see if you're heading in the right direction.

For example, if your product is a physical object and you want to evaluate visual appeal, start with a foam, wood, or clay model. Then, as you get more feedback, create a plastic model.

The type of feedback you want will often determine the type of prototype to create. If evaluators don't understand the prototype, it could be either the design or materials used. Keep evolving the prototype until you create one that evaluators like.

If you do not have the technical know-how to make a prototype, get in touch with a mechanical engineer, industrial engineer, electronic engineer, software engineer, programmer, or web designer (depending on your product type).

For an inexpensive place to start, contact your local university engineering department to find out if they'll design and build a prototype. Do not disclose the idea at first, just ask if they'd be willing to help with designs and prototypes.

Another place to find technical talent is through local chapters of major organizations such as:

- Institute of Electronic and Electrical Engineers (www.ieee.org)
- American Electronics Association (www.aeanet.org)
- American Society of Mechanical Engineers (www.asme.org)
- Society of Manufacturing Engineers (www.sme.org)
- Software and Information Industry Association (www.siia.net)

You don't need to know everything about the technology behind the prototype process, but it's good to be informed. To give you some insight about prototyping, the following prototype methods are explained.

Physical Objects

A physical prototype is used to evaluate a product's mechanical functionality and visual appeal. Examples include toys, tools, jewelry, and containers.

Physical prototypes are created by hand tools, machine tools, and by rapid prototyping techniques. They're made by either removing material (e.g., by drilling), or adding material (e.g., pouring a mold).

You can create a physical prototype by simply shaping an object by hand with tools (e.g., sawing, grinding, drilling, and milling). Start with a block of foam, wood, plastic, or metal and remove material until you get the desired look and feel.

An elaborate method for shaping an object involves using a computer-controlled milling machine. Known as Computer Numerical Control (CNC), the machine automatically shapes an object based on a computer-aided design or set of instructions. Use CNC when you need high accuracy for parts such as gears. A prototype project created by CNC can take two to three weeks, depending on its complexity.

If your prototype is made of metal, you have a few other methods from which to choose. A metal prototype can be made by casting, compacting, forging, or extrusion. Depending on the design and material, production could take from a week to a month.

You can make simple molds by shaping your object in clay and letting it harden. Then, after suspending it in a container with string or placing it on a support, pour liquid silicon into the container to cover half of the object. Let the first half of the silicon harden. Then, pour in additional silicon until the second half is covered. Let the second half of silicon harden. You now have two halves of a mold. Open the mold and remove the original clay object. Put the empty two halves of the silicon mold together and wrap it with rubber bands. Cut a small hole at the top and pour plastic resin into the mold. When the resin hardens you have a prototype.

Before advances in computers and materials, a complex prototype could take weeks or months to build. Today, the most technically advanced method to create a prototype is known as Rapid Prototyping (RP). With an RP machine, a prototype can be produced in a matter of hours.

RP was invented in 1988 with the introduction of Stereolithography by 3D Systems of Valencia, California. Rapid Prototyping machines literally create an object out of liquid resin, powder, or sheets of laminated paper. Costs for this process depend on the size and complexity of the object. A small prototype can start at $250. Costs increase for size, complexity, and painting or silk screening.

In general, RP is useful for showing a model to a focus group or trade representative. It also provides engineering proof of concept. The following are the leading methods used in Rapid Prototyping:

- **Stereolithography Apparatus** (SLA) – A process based on the use of photopolymer liquid resins that solidify when exposed to ultraviolet light. A software program transfers the designer's 3D CAD model into an electronic file for stereolithography machines ("STL" format), composing the information into thin cross-sections or layers. A laser beam then traces each layer onto the surface of a vat of photopolymer resin, building the part in repeated layers until a solid replica of the original CAD model is completed. SLA is one of the least expensive prototype methods and can be produced quickly. See 3D Systems (www.3dsystems.com) for more about SLA.
- **Selective Laser Sintering** (SLS) – A process that creates solid three-dimensional objects, layer by layer, from plastic, metal, or ceramic powders that are "sintered" or fused using carbon-dioxide laser energy. The inherent material versatility of SLS technology allows for a broader range of advanced rapid prototyping and manufacturing applications. SLS costs more than SLA, but is stronger, more durable, is heat resistant, and chemical resistant.
- **Fused Deposition Modeling** (FDM) – A process that creates successive cross-sections of a three-dimensional object from threads of plastic or casting wax. Similar to a hot glue gun, plastic is extruded through the modeler tip of the FDM machine. The FDM modeler head moves along both the x- and y-axis across a foundation and deposits a layer of material. This process continues until all layers of the part have been completed. FDM is not as

popular as SLA or SLS. See Stratasys for more about FDM (www.stratasys.com).

- **Laminated Object Manufacturing** (LOM) – A process that creates a three-dimensional object from layers of paper with a polyethylene coating on the backside. A sheet of paper is fed through the machine with the aid of small rollers. As the paper is fed through, steam is used to heat the paper's coating so that each new layer will adhere to the previous one. A carbon-dioxide laser then traces, or etches, the outline of the cross-sectional pattern into the top layer of paper. Once the laser has finished etching the pattern, it burns a border into the paper that contains the etched pattern. This enables the part to stay intact as each new layer is created. Since LOM parts are made from paper, humidity and temperature affect the structure. Therefore, lacquer is often added as a protective measure. Overall, LOM is very useful for creating large parts quickly.

- **3D Printing** – A process that creates a three-dimensional object using powder material. A type of ink-jet printing head selectively deposits or "prints" a binder fluid to fuse powder in designated areas. The platform is lowered, more powder added and leveled, and the process repeated. (Typical layer thickness is on the order of 0.1 mm.) This process is very fast, and produces parts with a slightly grainy surface. The finished part can be filled and coated with special types of resin, urethane, glue, or wax to improve its strength and durability. For more information about 3D Printing, see Z Corporation (www.zcorp.com).

The general process to produce a physical prototype is:

1. Search for an industrial designer or mechanical engineer who has experience with rapid prototyping. It's best if he or she uses leading CAD software like SolidWorks or Pro/ENGINEER.

2. Take your Prototype Requirements and sketches to an industrial designer or mechanical engineer. Request a price quote to produce a computer-aided design (CAD) of your object. If your prototype is produced on a computerized milling machine, a computer-aided manufacturing (CAM) design file is needed as well. A CAM file contains the x, y, and z coordinates needed to shape your prototype.

3. Search for a prototype company using the Internet or Yellow Pages under the heading of Prototype or Product Developing. One of the largest prototype makers is Arrk Product Development Group (www.arrk.com).

4. Ask the prototype company to sign your non-disclosure agreement.

5. Provide the prototype company with a CD of your CAD files and Prototype Requirements. Request a price quote and completion time. They'll usually ask for your budget as a guide to what they can offer.

6. Upon agreement, the prototype company will begin the process by converting your CAD files into files needed to control their machines, and then create the prototype.

Physical prototypes can also be demonstrated through computer animation, which represents objects with a series of three-dimensional computer-aided designs. Animation software uses your designs to create virtual prototypes that display form and function. Instead of handing someone an object to examine, the prototype is displayed on a computer monitor or output to videotape. This method is an especially useful alternative when complex and expensive prototypes are involved.

Electronic Devices

Electronic prototypes are used to test the functionality of your electronic invention. They don't have to look pretty, they just need to function according to specifications.

An electronic engineer can design a circuit on paper or with a computer design tool. Once the design is created, electronic parts are laid out and connected to form a circuit. Here are the major methods for assembling an electronic prototype:

- **Breadboards** – A device with rows and columns of connections allowing circuits to be designed and tested. They're best for simple designs of low-frequency analog or digital circuits.
- **Wirewrap** – A method of making circuit connections by wrapping wire from the socket of one part to another. This is a quick and easy method for making reliable connections.
- **Perfboards** – A fiberglass board with a grid of pre-drilled holes that houses electronic parts. Electronic parts are placed onto the board with their leads fed through the holes. The leads are either soldered or twisted together with other parts. The connections are not always reliable but may be fine for a small project.
- **Printed circuit boards** – A method of making circuit connections by etching a copper diagram on a fiberglass board. This method uses chemicals to form the printed circuit board (PCB). Holes are drilled along the copper lines to place the electronic parts. The parts are positioned on the board and soldered in place. This method is more costly and is used as a refining step after a breadboard, wirewrap, or perfboard prototype.

Start with a breadboard or wirewrap prototype to prove the function of the circuit design. Note that certain high-frequency circuits do not work well on a breadboard. Therefore you'll probably need to build the prototype from a printed circuit board.

You can also design and demonstrate an electronic prototype with simulated circuit design software. The software helps you layout the design and test with simulated inputs and outputs. This method might provide enough information for evaluators to offer feedback. Once you've proved that a design works, develop a circuit and continue testing it under various conditions similar to that of the final product.

Software and Websites

There are two reasons to prototype software and websites. One is to evaluate the visual appeal and the other is to test the functionality. The visual element is what users see and interact with (e.g., clicking buttons, choosing items from a list). The functional element is how the software will work behind the scene (e.g., database processing, bill paying).

Two prototyping methods capture the visual aspect of software and websites: paper sketches and screens. Paper sketches are best for early designs for feedback on content and where objects are placed. Interactive screens work best for mature prototypes.

Paper sketches are simply sheets of paper with handwritten objects to show the interface to potential users. Arrange sketches on several pages so they mimic the way a user would normally interact with the software or website. Paper sketches will give evaluators the sense that the design is not set and may be easily changed. This allows them to offer creative solutions.

When presenting a layout already on a screen, evaluators tend to respond as if the design is less likely to change. This may inhibit feedback.

As the design matures, create screen designs using visual tools such as Microsoft VisualBasic or Macromedia Dreamweaver. These tools allow visual objects to be created and placed quickly for on-screen evaluation.

Functionality evaluation of software and websites is performed in steps. The first step involves drawing flowcharts, diagrams, or outlines to show the work process. This is done on a whiteboard, paper, or on the computer using Word, Excel, or other organizing software. Then, source code is developed in tandem with the visual elements. In addition, test cases are created to examine the results of various scenarios.

Prototype Summary

Which type of prototype is best will depend on your goals, budget, and the complexity of the object. Determining how your final product will be produced will help you choose the best prototype method. When the time comes to produce your product, it will save time and money if you use the same or similar tools for making the prototype.

To find a manufacturer to build your prototype, talk to business and technical contacts in your community for recommendations. In addition, use the Internet by searching with terms ["your product type" and "manufacturer"] or ["your product type" and "prototype"]. Contact manufacturers and ask if they build prototypes. Send manufacturers your requirements and have them send you a quote on the cost to produce a prototype. It's also a good idea to ask the manufacturer to sign a non-disclosure agreement before you send the requirements. Of the quotes that are within your budget, ask to meet the manufacturer to get a tour of the facility and discuss the details of your product. Select the manufacturer that you think will be the easiest to work with. Negotiate on price and time it will take to finish the prototype. Approve the order to go forward. When the prototype is made, check that it conforms to your requirements before you sign-off and pay the invoice. If there are flaws, ask to have them corrected.

VALIDATE YOUR PROTOTYPE

Now that you have a prototype, it's time to get feedback. You'll want to make sure that your prototype solves a problem or satisfies a need or want, and does it better than other products. Feedback will let you know what potential customers are looking for when selecting your type of product. At this point, you'll need to validate features and functionality, uncover possible product shortcomings, and discover areas for improvement.

In addition to prototype features and functions, you'll want to learn what motivates and drives customer purchases. This information will help you establish price points and create marketing and sales strategies.

Keep in mind that an interview is not necessarily a one-time thing. You may have a series of interviews, prototype refinement, and then another series of interviews for fine-tuning. Your interviews can be conducted with formal focus groups or with relatively informal individual or small groups.

A focus group interview typically involves a formal script designed in advance by a professional researcher. The actual focus group, conducted by a professional moderator, takes place behind a one-way mirror so that you can observe the dynamics. Focus groups are also videotaped for later analysis.

You can do the interviewing yourself or hire a marketing consultant or agency to create a plan, recruit attendees, and lead a discussion. An agency might charge as much as five to ten thousand dollars to organize and conduct a focus group. You can do it yourself by using the following steps:

- Create an interview plan
- Recruit candidates
- Ask prepared questions
- Summarize the feedback

Prototype Interview Plan

To help guide the process of obtaining prototype feedback, start by creating a simple plan. A prototype interview plan outlines your goals, objectives, who you want to interview, budget, questions to ask, and how you'll conduct the meetings. The entire plan can be as short as one or two pages. By planning now, you'll be focused and as a result, save time. Use the template on the following page as a guide.

Prototype Interview Plan

Before interviewing people for feedback on your prototype, create a plan using this template as a guide.

Goals and Objectives
Type of feedback you seek (e.g., ease of use, functionality, industrial design, does your idea solve a problem).

Participant Profile
Profile of participants you want to evaluate your prototype (e.g., age, income level, job title).

Participant Experience
Level of experience an evaluator should have (e.g., uses similar product daily for at least five years).

Group Size
Number of groups and size of each (e.g., one-on-one, six groups of five people each).

Recruitment
Methods and places you'll look for people (e.g., user groups, club members, unions).

Budget
The amount you can spend for interviewing (e.g., costs of meeting room, travel, interviewee compensation such as cash or free lunch).

Meetings
The meeting place and duration of each meeting (e.g., office conference room for two hours).

Materials
Materials needed (e.g., prototypes, audio recorder, video recorder, white board, paper, pencils, refreshments).

Questions
The questions you'll ask (e.g., What's important when choosing this type of product?).

Recruit Attendees

Recruit people who have some experience with the type of product you're creating. For example, if your product were a new gardening tool, you'd recruit people who use gardening tools as either hobbyists or professionals, depending on your target market.

Recruit people from a variety of sources. Consider using people who have previously participated in one of your surveys. Tap those who currently use a product that you hope to replace or improve. Some of these people might be part of a special interest group that has meetings that focus on your product type. For example, if your product is computer software, there are groups that meet to discuss graphics, security, and game software. Visit these groups to ask if they are open to evaluating your product at a later time.

If your idea is a common household product, talk with friends, relatives, neighbors, and other associates. Attend trade shows or conferences to talk with buyers and sellers. If recruiting people is difficult, use a marketing company that specializes in interviews or focus groups to recruit for you. They usually have a database of people available for product interviews.

How many people should be interviewed? Typically, a minimum sample size of 30 is preferred, while each group should not include more than five to ten people at a time. But, the greater and more diverse the people you talk with, the better. Recruit from each of your possible market segments to get a range of feedback, and also to discover which segment is most interested.

You may interview people one-on-one or in small groups. People tend to respond synergistically and become more creative in small groups. But it's also possible that some people will unintentionally dominate and suppress others. Your job entails making sure that everyone gets heard by requesting feedback from those who have not had a chance to contribute.

You'll also need to determine an incentive for luring someone to the meeting. People generally want something in return for their time. Often a cash incentive is effective, but lunch, dinner, or snacks also work. Before you officially recruit your respondents, ask what would persuade them to participate.

If you suspect your discussions may give away product secrets, ask people to sign a non-disclosure agreement (NDA). The NDA provides limited protection against people disclosing confidential information to others or building your product themselves. You can find NDA forms on the Internet or you may use the sample in Appendix G. Ask an attorney to review an NDA to make sure it suits your needs.

Ask Prepared Questions

You'll need to develop questions that will provide useful feedback. You'll ask general questions and then questions specifically about your prototype.

You'll need to be open to and prepared for negative feedback. Do not argue or try to defend yourself. If evaluators don't like your prototype, let them know you'll take their suggestions into consideration.

The meeting place can be in a conference room, a home, or outdoors. The setting should be comfortable and in a place where your product type is normally used. At the beginning of your interview, thank attendees for participating and ask them to briefly identify themselves. Reinforce that you are not selling anything, but are conducting research for a new product idea.

It will be helpful to document the session with audio or video equipment, so let attendees know they're being recorded and that these recordings are for research purposes only.

Tell them the type of product you are working on. But, prior to showing the prototype, ask the following type of questions and record the answers:

- What is your experience with this type of product?
- If there were one thing you wish your current product could do better, what would it be?

- When using that product, is it ____ (fast enough, easy to use, small enough, efficient, cost effective)?
- When using that product, does it ____ (break down often, wear out, leak, crash often, produce the wrong results, act unreliably)?
- What features and benefits do you look for when choosing this type of product?
- What is more important to you: product quality, functionality, customer service, warranty, or price?
- What would it take for you to switch to a new product?

When asking questions:

- Do not tell them the typical problem your prototype solves, let them tell you their problems.
- Do not tell how great your prototype is, let them tell you if it is.
- Do not settle for yes or no answers. Delve into why they answered the way they did.

Next, reveal your prototype. Demonstrate its functions and point out features. Let attendees examine and use it. Ask the following questions:

- How well do you think the prototype will solve your problem or satisfy your needs and wants?
- Do you think this is an improvement over existing products?
- What do you think are the key advantages over other products?
- How do you like the colors, shapes, functions, etc.?
- How much would be too much to spend on the finished product?

Watching someone use your product is valuable information. Have evaluators perform a task scenario and see how well they do it. For example, if your product were a new gardening tool to prune flowers, you'd ask them to perform this task and notice if they operated the tool as intended.

Feedback Summary

At the end of the interview, ask them to fill out a brief survey. Remember to reinforce the fact that their feedback is valuable and will be kept private.

Sample Prototype Evaluation Survey

Your opinions are very much appreciated. Please answer the following questions.

1. Do you have a need or want related to the product type mentioned?
❑ Always ❑ Most of the time ❑ Sometimes ❑ Rarely ❑ Never

2. How well do you think the finished product will meet your needs?
❑ Excellent ❑ Very Good ❑ Somewhat ❑ Poor ❑ Not at all

3. If this product was available, and the price was reasonable, would you likely purchase a product like this for yourself or as a gift (you are not under any obligation to do so)?
❑ Definitely ❑ Very likely ❑ Somewhat ❑ Unlikely ❑ Not at all

4. Would you recommend this product to someone else?
❑ Definitely ❑ Very likely ❑ Somewhat ❑ Unlikely ❑ Not at all

What do you like about the prototype?

What do you dislike about the prototype?

Please state some suggestions for improvement:

Thank you for your time!

The answers you receive will help shape your product. In addition, they'll provide a foundation for your marketing communications. If a majority of the people you talk with are satisfied with their existing product, and your product idea offers no significant advantages, you'll probably want to reevaluate your invention. On the other hand, you may uncover a significant percentage of people who are either dissatisfied with their current product or are looking for something better. In that case, you are on to something.

Prototype Feedback Summary

At the end of each meeting, summarize the interview discussions and evaluation surveys by answering the following.

Summarize
Demographics of people surveyed:

Problems, needs, and wants solved by your prototype:

What they liked about the prototype:

What they did not like about the prototype:

How the prototype was used differently than expected:

Key suggestions given:

Scores
Number of people surveyed:

Number of surveys with top scores:

Percentage of surveys with top scores:

Decision Path Three

This is the third and final Decision Path exercise. The Decision Path is a quick review to see if your idea makes sense so far. For each of the following questions, circle "**Yes**" or "**No**." If you're not sure of the answer, circle the "**?**" question mark.

Decision Path Three
1. Have you received favorable results from your Interview or Market Test (at least 80% of those surveyed have given the idea top scores such as Excellent or Very Good)?   Yes   No   ?
2. Do your customers perceive your product as a better solution than the competition?   Yes   No   ?
3. Can the competition be overcome in terms of product, marketing, and sales strategies?   Yes   No   ?
4. Will you receive adequate funding to develop, market, and sell your product?   Yes   No   ?
5. Will you have the people lined up to develop, market, and sell your product?   Yes   No   ?

If you answered "Yes" to all of these questions, you're on the right track and can continue. If you have a mix of "Yes" and "No" answers, then revise the idea or conduct more research into those questions. If most or all your answers are "No," then it might be best to cancel this project. If you answered "?" to a few questions, get the answers before moving to the next step.

I compliment you on your creativity and diligence for getting this far. Please continue.

Chapter 13
Patent Review

At this point, you've performed a preliminary patent search and also determined that your invention is marketable. Now it's time to perform a detailed search of patents and publications in the public domain (also known as "prior art"). The patent search accomplishes two things. First, it helps ensure that your product won't infringe on an active patent, and second, reveals if you can protect your invention with a patent.

People have successfully searched and filed patents themselves. You can do this, but it'll take a lot of time and effort. I recommend performing a patent search yourself and then follow-up with a patent attorney. Find a patent attorney who has experience with your product type to help you search and then file an application. You can save some money by providing a list of patents similar to your invention. And, while most patent attorneys are thorough, you know your invention better than anyone else does. Providing a list of similar patents will increase the possibility of uncovering relevant patents they might not have considered.

Since you cannot patent something that has already been patented, you'll need to search for relevant patents. The time period to search for patents is generally since the beginning of a particular technology.

On the other hand, to determine if you might infringe on a patent, you need to review only currently active patents (i.e., typically the last 20 years).

To summarize the differences between a patentability search and infringement search, the following guide outlines the time period and parts of a patent to review.

Patent Search Guide		
	Search Time Period	Examine
Patentability Search	Search all patents dated as far back as to when a particular technology began.	Review an entire patent to determine if your invention is unique compared to any previous patent.
Infringement Search	Search all active patents, which go back 20 years for utility patents, or 14 years for design and plant patents.	Review the Claims section of a patent to determine if it includes all the aspects of your invention.

Currently, the United States Patent and Trademark Office (USPTO) provides a free patent search (www.uspto.gov). There are alternative websites for patent searching, but the USPTO website is your best source. Also, some universities and public libraries (known as Patent and Trademark Depository Libraries) offer free patent search workstations. They use a CD or DVD system, but may not include the most current patents. Again, the USPTO website is your best source.

If you think that you'll market your product in Europe, search the European Patent Office website, which also includes Japanese patents (www.epo.org). And if you think you might introduce your product in Canada, search the Canadian Intellectual Property Office website (cipo.gc.ca).

What to Look For

A United States Patent includes the Patent Number, Inventor, Date of Patent, Classifications, References, Abstract, Background, Summary, Drawings, Description of Drawings, and Claims.

First, read the Abstract. The Abstract is a short overview of the patent. If the description of the invention mentioned in the Abstract is similar to yours, log the Patent Number, Patent Name, Class, and Date of Patent using the template provided in this chapter or create your own.

The section of a patent that's examined for infringement is the Claims section. The Claims are specific attributes that make a particular patent unique. When you've completed your search, review the Claims section of any patent that appears similar to your product idea. Again, you're best off retaining a patent attorney to review Claims and provide a written opinion concerning possible infringement.

Note that the patent system is organized into classifications and subclassifications. Once you find the classification that closely matches your invention, you can focus your search on patents that are in the same classification and subclass. Eventually, your invention will fall into a classification determined by the patent examiner. But when you file for a patent, the application requires you to list classifications of patents you searched.

Patent Search Methods

To keep a patent search simple, I'll focus on methods to search the USPTO website, but these techniques could be applied to other patent databases. Websites often change, so actual procedures might differ among databases. Here are the steps for quickly searching patents:

```
┌─────────────────────────────────────────────────────┐
│              USPTO Quick Search                      │
├─────────────────────────────────────────────────────┤
│ This is a representation of the Quick Search screen  │
│ at the USPTO website.                                │
│                                                      │
│ Query                                                │
│   Term 1: [            ]  in Field 1: [ All Fields ▼]│
│                                                      │
│                                                      │
│   Term 2: [            ]  in Field 2: [ All Fields ▼]│
│                                                      │
│ Select Years                                         │
│ [ 1976 to Present (full-text) ▼ ]    [  Search  ]   │
└─────────────────────────────────────────────────────┘
```

1. Think of commonly used words pertaining to the function or description your invention. These are known as keywords. You'll use the keywords to perform a search. From the USPTO homepage, click on Patents, then Search Patents, and then Quick Search. Type a keyword or keyword phrase where it says *Query Term 1* and click the Search button. For example, in *Query Term 1* enter "locking mechanism" and in *Field 1* keep the setting "All Fields" and click the Search button.

2. If there's a match, you'll be given a list of found patents. If you get over a hundred patents, go back and enter more specific keywords (e.g., "seatbelt locking mechanism"). But if you get only a few patents, go back and enter more general keywords.

3. The list includes the Patent Number and Title links. Click on the Patent Number link to display the patent. Read the Abstract and if the description is similar to your product idea, log the patent number, name, classification, and date. In addition, look at the drawings to get a better feel for similarity or not. While viewing a

patent, click on the Images link to display the complete patent along with drawings.

4. Now, search by classification. Using the Quick Search, enter a classification and subclass that you found from searching patents by keywords. In *Query Term 1* enter a classification number and in *Field 1* click on the menu list for "Current US Classification" and then click the Search button.

5. You'll receive a list of patents based on the classification and subclass you entered. Again, click on the Patent Number link and read the Abstract. If the description is similar to your invention, log the patent number, name, class, and date.

Here are some forms to help you track your patent search.

Patent Search Log			
Patent Number	Patent Name	Patent Class/Subclass	Date of Patent

Keyword Search Log
Keep track of keywords used in your patent search (e.g., bicycle, ball joint, locking mechanism).

Keywords that uncovered relevant patents:

Keywords that did not uncover relevant patents:
 |

Search Periodicals

The technology or method that embodies your invention may also have appeared in a research journal, magazine article, website, or advertisement. Look for these with an Internet search engine such as Google or periodical database such as InfoTrac found at a library. If something looks similar to your invention, save and print the entire item, and then consult a patent attorney for an opinion.

Periodicals Search Log			
Publication Name or Website	Date	Article Title or Ad Headline	Author or Company

Patents That Match Your Invention

If you uncover a patent that's the same as your invention, it does not necessarily mean the game is over. There might be enough innovation in your design to warrant a new patent. Some patent attorneys are trained to modify your invention to avoid infringement and / or to obtain a patent. If anything looks identical, discuss it with a patent attorney.

Chapter 14
Self-Market or License

Don't let adverse facts stand in the way of a good decision.

Colin Powell

By now you believe that your product idea is marketable. But which is best – self-marketing or licensing? If you self-market, there's the excitement of running your own business. At the same time, you have business expenses to contend with and the responsibility of generating a positive cash flow. You must be committed and have passion to succeed.

Many people make the mistake of quitting their job to start a business. It may take six months or more before a new business can generate a salary and a profit.

If you cannot afford to go without a paycheck and cannot work part-time building a business, licensing may be the way to go. Also, licensing your product will give you free time to work on other ideas. Whether you decide to self-market or license, your product idea should:

- Have a specific advantage over the competition
- Have received favorable feedback
- Pass all regulatory certifications and compliance issues (if required)

Self-Marketing vs. Licensing Example

Here is a sample financial comparison of self-marketing versus licensing:

Background

- Unit costs to manufacture and package = $25
- Product retail selling price = $100
- Number of units sold = 20,000
- Product Sales = $2,000,000

Licensing Royalty

Assumption:
- Royalty = 5% of Product Sales

Licensing Royalty   = Royalty percentage x Product Sales
                    = 5% x $2,000,000
                    = $100,000

Self-Marketing Profit

Assumptions:
- Startup expenses = $50,000
- Operational, Marketing, and Sales expenses = $150,000

Gross Profit   = Product Sales – (Unit cost x Units sold)
               = $2,000,000 – ($25 x 20,000)
               = $2,000,000 – $500,000
               = $1,500,000

Net Profit   = Gross Profit – Expenses
             = $1,500,000 – ($50,000 + $150,000)
             = $1,500,000 – $200,000
             = $1,300,000

In this example, the self-marketer earned $1,300,000 versus $100,000 by licensing. The self-marketer made more money, but that's after investing his or her own money to get started and putting in many hours per week.

An advantage to the self-marketer is that the business can be sold and proceeds invested to generate a future cash flow. On the other hand, the licensor may make less, but will have more free time to work on other ideas. As you were reading this scenario, did you see yourself as the self-marketer or licensor?

Is Self-Marketing for You?

To get a feel whether self-marketing is for you, select either "**Yes**" or "**No**" for the following questions:

Self-Marketing Decision		
1. Do you want to build a business around your idea?	Yes	No
2. Do you have or can you raise money to cover business expenses?	Yes	No
3. Are you skilled at organizing and planning?	Yes	No
4. If you're working, do you have spare time to build your business on the side?	Yes	No
5. If you're working and want to quit your job, do you have reserves to pay your living expenses and business expenses for at least six months?	Yes	No
6. Can you find mentors to advise you in areas that are not your strengths?	Yes	No
7. Do you have knowledge of the industry related to your product idea?	Yes	No

❏ Check here if you answered "Yes" to all the self-marketing questions. If so, self-marketing is for you.

Is Licensing for You?

To get a feel whether licensing is for you, select either "**Yes**" or "**No**" for the following questions:

Licensing Decision		
1. Do you want to license your product?	Yes	No
2. Can you present a forecast that shows your product will earn a profit for a licensing company in its first year?	Yes	No
3. Can the product be patented?	Yes	No
4. Are you willing to learn how to find the right company to license, present the benefits of your product, and negotiate the terms of a contract? If not, are you willing to use an Agent and take less of a royalty?	Yes	No

❑ Check here if you answered "Yes" to all the licensing questions. If you did, licensing is for you.

Decision Path A or B

Now it's time to make a decision. If you're hesitant, get opinions from people who have been through self-marketing and licensing. Which do you choose?

❑ Self-market (Path A)
❑ License (Path B)
❑ Not sure

If you selected licensing, follow the steps in the "Licensing Your Idea" chapter. If you selected self-marketing or are still not sure, continue with the next chapter.

Part Three
DEVELOPMENT & LAUNCH

Obstacles cannot crush me. Every obstacle yields to stern resolve. He who is fixed to a star does not change his mind.
Leonardo da Vinci

Step Four – Plan It
Step Five – Develop It
Step Six – Launch It
Post-Launch Progress Check

Chapter 15
Step Four – Plan It

First comes thought; then organization of that thought, into ideas and plans; then transformation of those plans into reality. The beginning, as you will observe, is in your imagination.

Napoleon Hill

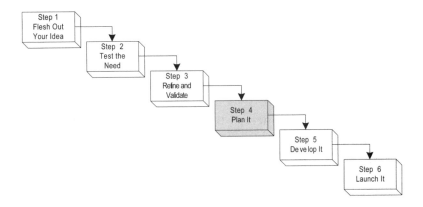

The fourth step of the **Market-Step** process is planning. Planning involves completely thinking through product marketing and development details from start to finish. This is a key step to taking your invention and turning it into a product. Detailed planning can seem arduous, but clear plans lead to greater product quality and shorter development time. The closer you get to producing your product, the more costly changes become. So, you'll want to uncover any remaining issues now before full development begins.

If you need to present a formal product plan to an investor, licensor, supervisor, or partner, see "Market-Step Product Plan" in Appendix C. Even if you don't need a formal plan, put your thoughts on paper anyway.

In Step Four you'll focus on:

Market Planning
1. Evaluating positioning
2. Determining a price
3. Planning marketing communications
4. Determining distribution
5. Reviewing regulations and certifications

Development Planning
6. Creating product requirements
7. Creating a manufacturing plan
8. Creating a project plan
9. Creating a launch checklist
10. Setting a budget

If you're completing Step Four yourself, perform activities one through ten in sequence. If you have two or more people, you can save time by working in tandem. A person or team can take on Market Planning and the other Development Planning.

MARKET PLANNING

Product Positioning

Positioning is a powerful concept. Positioning tells people what your product does and how well it does it. With all of the noise in the market, your product needs to stand out amid the competition. Your product needs to have a clear identity.

Think of your product from your customers' perspective. Customers seek benefits. Your product must represent a way to make money, save money, save time, gain recognition, or provide safety.

Step Four – Development Planning Flowchart

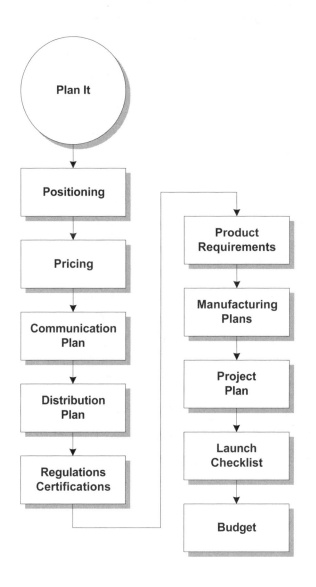

People want to understand how your product compares to the competition. Is your product more expensive or less expensive? Does it offer the best value? Is it the market leader, the most dependable, the most convenient, the easiest to use, the most comfortable, and so on?

For example, when it comes to cars, Volvo is synonymous with safety. Advertising focuses on safety, which reinforces this positioning. In addition, Volvo is positioned as more expensive, that reinforces perceptions of quality and safety.

Over ten years ago, Hertz was number one and Avis was a distant second in the car rental market. Then, Avis came right out and said in its advertisements, "We're Number 2. We try harder." As a result, people figured Avis would make every possible effort to give its customers good deals and great service. Whether Avis really does try harder is not known, nor does it matter. The positioning worked.

Positioning helps customers identify with your product and is a means for setting product expectations. Positioning provides a foundation for all communications including advertising, press releases, packaging, and the product name itself.

But just stating the product has a certain position is not enough. If you position your product as reliable and it falls apart, you lose credibility and customers. You can say you're the best product, but you'll need to back it up with quality and service. In other words, the product must perform as stated.

One way to determine positioning involves charting all the products in the market in terms of value to the customer. In this case, value is defined as price combined with the capabilities (benefits and features) that customers want. First, position each competitor on the chart based on selling price and capabilities. Then, look for openings on the chart that might provide opportunities to stand out from the crowd.

The following chart looks at three products in the market (Product A, B, and C) in terms of price and capability. The charting of these products was used to look for gaps in the market. And then to create a product that provides more value to the customer (fills the gap). The observations are:

- Compared to Product A, New Product is the same price but has more capabilities.
- Compared to Product B, New Product is less expensive and has more capabilities.
- Compared to Product C, New Product is less expensive for the same capabilities.
- Overall, from this chart, New Product offers the best value in terms of price and capability.

Sample Positioning of Competitors

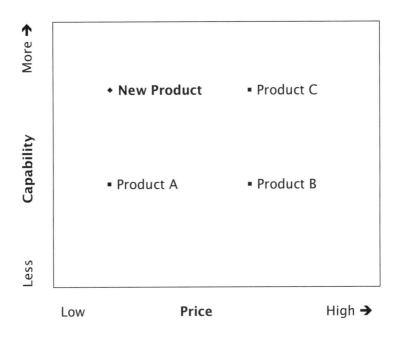

Chart the position of your direct competitors and similar products in terms of price and capabilities customers want. Look for opportunities in the market to serve your customers with greater value. Keep in mind that capabilities may include better customer service, ease of use, or greater product availability. For more information, see "Investigate Your Competition" in Appendix A.

Pricing for Profit

Pricing is one of the most difficult product decisions you'll make. There's no magic formula for perfect pricing, but I'll offer some guidance to narrow your price within a range.

Your retail price should fall somewhere between the highest amount customers are willing to pay and an amount that covers your costs and expenses. In general, most retail products are priced within an average competitor price for a particular product class. And, how your product compares to the competition will influence whether your price should be above or below the average.

Setting a Price Point
$$$ The Upper Limit The most customers are willing to pay
$$ Middle Average competitive price
$ The Lower Limit Product costs and expenses

The Most Customers Are Willing to Pay

The highest your product can be priced is based on what customers are willing to pay. Get feedback from potential customers, distributors, and retailers. Ask them, "What's considered too expensive for this product?" The typical amount they tell you is the upper limit. Also, read Internet discussions to see what people are saying about price for your product type.

If your product is a specialty item containing rare materials or superior sophistication, then set a high price. Or, if you have a unique product that's sought after and there are no competitors, price it very high in the beginning. You can drop your price as needed to meet the competition. For example, years ago there was a software program that manipulated graphic images in record time. No other product like it existed and the company charged $500 and generated large profits. Eventually, other products came along and did the same thing for a lot less. The company then lowered their price.

If your product is for business end-users, keep in mind they are usually less price sensitive than consumers. Businesses conclude that quality products, which lead to increased productivity, are cost effective. If you can quantify the fact that your product will save money, make money, or save time, then a business will become interested.

The amount you may charge depends on the value customers will derive. Let's assume your product saves two hours of labor every workday, which translates into a $5,000 savings per year. In this case, the customer may be happy to spend $1,000 to get five times the cost savings.

Average Competitive Price

If customers perceive your product as high quality and offering advantages over the competition, go ahead and set your price above the average competitive price. You can charge higher prices if you can provide faster service, a money-back guarantee, and great customer support. But, you must communicate that you offer these advantages.

If your marketing budget is higher than the competition's, then that is another reason to set a price higher than the average competitive price. If, for example, you run television, radio, and magazine advertising, while the competition does not, your costs will be greater, but you'll have a stronger chance of reaching and influencing more people.

Product Costs and Expenses

The lowest possible selling price must be at a point where you can still generate a profit. The lowest price you can charge, on average, is based on your product unit costs, expenses, and profit goals. If you sell through a distributor, then remember to determine your profit based on the distributor's price, not the retail price. Here's how to calculate profit:

- Gross Profit = (Selling Price x Units sold) – (Unit cost x Units sold)
- Net Profit = Gross Profit – Expenses

Use a spreadsheet to calculate profit using various selling prices, number of units you can sell, and expenses. And, calculate profit when you have a mix of direct sales and sales through distribution. If you're not sure about your numbers, talk to an accountant or product specialist for guidance. For more financial information, see "Product Math" in Appendix D. Also, you can find spreadsheet templates that complement this book at my website (www.MattYubas.com).

Shopping Styles

You'll also need to consider how your typical buyer shops when pricing your product. Roper Starch, a market research company, conducted a recent worldwide survey of 40,000 people and concluded that shoppers come in four styles. For the most part, buyers are either:

- **Innovators** – 21% buy the latest innovative product. Innovators want the latest gadget and will pay almost any price. If your product is cutting edge, cool, and creative, then innovators want your product. Set a high price when you launch your product.
- **Deal Makers** – 29% love the buying process itself. Deal Makers research, compare prices, and look for value. If your product offers a good solution at a competitive price, you can win many sales. To win over the Deal Makers, set your retail price within 10% to 20% of the average competitive price depending on the advantages and quality of your product.

- **Price Seekers** – 27% indicate that price is the most important consideration. Price Seekers want the lowest price because they only want a basic product that gets the job done. They often buy generic non-brands or wait for sales. You can make a profit with the lowest price if you keep costs and expenses to a minimum.
- **Brand Loyalists** – 23% buy mostly name brands. Brand Loyalists want a name brand they can trust. They are willing to pay higher prices with the expectation of quality. If there are no brand name competitors for your type of product, you can capture these people with professional-looking brochures and nice packaging, emphasizing quality in your messages. In this case, set a higher-than-average price to attract brand loyalists. If brand names exist in your market, you'll either have to build a brand name with a lot of marketing, or lower your price to appeal to Deal Makers and Price Seekers.

Your product won't appeal to everyone, so think about which group of shoppers your product will attract, and set the price accordingly.

Quantity Discounts

People expect a price break when buying in quantity. Discounts will vary depending on industry norms, competition, and profit potential. If your product sells in quantity such as packages of pens, film, or batteries, then provide quantity discounts. A quantity discount pricing structure to consider is the ratio of 1:2:5.

An increasing percent discount is offered with the larger the purchase. For example, a quantity of 10 items receives a 5% discount, 20 items a 10% discount, and 50 items a 15% discount. The quantity level can be any sequence of 1:2:5. For example, quantity discounts might be for 5, 10, 20, 50, 100, 200, and 500 items (5:1:2:5:1:2:5). When you create a discount program, be sure that at the highest discount, there is still room for profit.

Consumables

A product can be a combination of product plus a consumable element. For example, ink jet printers from HP and Epson are relatively inexpensive. The real money is in the consumable ink cartridges. Each cartridge sells for somewhere between 10% to 20% of the printer's selling price. Another example is selling a razor as the base product, and then selling blades as the consumable. A pricing strategy for a product plus a consumable involves offering the base product at an inexpensive price, and then making most of the profit with a high-priced consumable. The key here is designing your product so that your consumables are compatible with only your product.

You might try offering your consumables on a subscription basis. For example, the water-dispensing machine is low priced or free, but the containers of water must be purchased monthly. This provides recurring revenue you can count on as long as you maintain quality products and service.

Pricing Considerations

Other pricing considerations include seasonal market demands. On Valentine's Day the price of roses increases. Notice if you're able to raise prices or if you need to lower prices during certain times of the year. Notice also the consumer reaction as you raise or lower prices. Does a price change affect sales volume and therefore overall revenue?

Play with prices to see if total sales increase. If you're not sure, advertise your product with different prices in three similar magazines. See which brings in more sales. I once heard a successful jeweler say that if something does not sell, then raise the price.

New competitors will always appear with lower prices and new features. You'll have to stay ahead by listening to your customers and offering new features. Competitors that offer an inferior product might be going after a different market segment, and you can maintain your price. If they offer a similar quality product and service, you might need to drop your price depending on your positioning.

You can lower your price and still remain profitable by lowering your costs. Cut costs by buying larger quantities of supplies at a discount, finding cheaper or more efficient labor, and using less expensive packaging. Also, you might find that customers don't really need the high quality you offer. In this case, cut costs by using less-expensive product materials.

Marketing Communications Plan

Communications are used to inform, influence, and encourage. Though sometimes thought of as just advertising and promotion, a communications plan is the use of all possible mediums to make future customers aware of your business and product. You'll need to develop a communications plan that's designed to raise awareness, produce sales leads, generate interest, and motivate purchases.

Any transaction between sellers and buyers begins with awareness of your product. Awareness is created with marketing communications programs such as:

- Advertising
- Direct mail
- Direct email
- Magazine articles
- Newsletters
- Personal networking
- Product reviews
- Press releases
- Speaking appearances
- Trade shows

Awareness stimulates buyers, motivating them to get more information about your product. Buyers will investigate your product further by:

- Calling you
- Sending you email
- Returning a direct mail postcard
- Searching for product reviews or discussions
- Talking to existing customers
- Talking to opinion leaders
- Visiting a retailer
- Visiting your website

You have to convince customers that your product is the solution to their needs. Since people can be skeptical at first, provide testimonials of satisfied customers, beta testers, or product reviewers. Show lab test results, certifications, or survey results. You can influence a buyer's investigation by:

- Offering free samples, free trial periods, low introductory special price, or free shipping
- Designing packaging that stands out and clearly explains the product and how it benefits the customer
- Including a risk-free money-back satisfaction guarantee
- Launching a website that educates and informs plus offers time-oriented special offers
- Providing excellent customer service with prompt and accurate information

You can influence purchasing decisions with attractive brochures, packaging, etc. If buyers are interested, they'll investigate your product, weigh its pros and cons, and then make a purchase decision.

Talk to retailers, distributors, and marketing consultants to find out which communications methods have successfully generated sales for your type of product. Study how competitors market and sell their products. If they're successful, model a similar approach.

The diagram on the next page summarizes marketing programs available to create awareness and influence the customer's buying process.

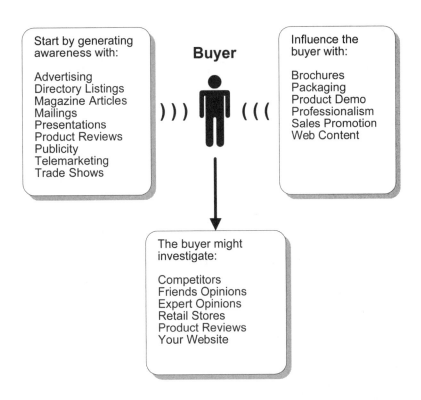

You're always better off using an integrated approach rather than putting all your money into one tactic. Using all the marketing tactics at your disposal – e.g., press releases, trade shows, and advertising—will give potential customers opportunities to learn about you from multiple sources.

Your marketing communications plan does not have to be complicated. A simple, yet effective, communications plan to launch a product could simply involve:

1. Submitting a product for trade magazine reviews
2. Placing advertisements in trade magazines
3. Issuing a press release when the product is available

4. Purchasing a list of names from trade magazines and sending direct mail to the subscribers, and then following-up responses with a telephone call
5. Buying search engine keywords to drive traffic to your website

You might, for example, begin by submitting articles and press releases to relevant trade magazines. Not only is this a relatively inexpensive way to start, but people tend to believe news and articles before they'll believe advertising. If you are not sure where to start, look at the marketing programs used by successful competitors.

Marketing Communication Tools

Check off the marketing communication tools other companies have used for your type of product (✓):

❑ Articles in magazines	❑ Packaging
❑ Billboards	❑ Posters
❑ Brochures	❑ Presentations
❑ Catalogs	❑ Press Kits
❑ Contests	❑ Product Launch Kits
❑ Coupons	❑ Product Reviews
❑ Datasheet	❑ Radio Ads
❑ Direct Email	❑ Seminars
❑ Direct Mail	❑ Speeches
❑ Flyers	❑ Technical Papers
❑ Internet Banner Ads	❑ Television Ads
❑ Magazine Ads	❑ Trade Shows
❑ Newsletters	❑ Website (yours, others)
❑ Newspaper Ads	❑ Yellow Pages

Even if your product sells in a retail store, you'll need to help generate awareness and interest. Discuss with the retailer how you can work together to increase revenue.

Let's say your product is a fishing lure. You buy a list of names from a fishing magazine. You send a postcard to all the people of the list. You have a great discount offer while boasting the benefits of your lure. The postcard directs people to local retailers that sell fishing equipment. The buyer walks into the retailer, shows the postcard to a store person, and is directed to the fishing lure section. Your fishing lure is packaged with a benefit message of catching more fish and offers a money-back guarantee. The buyer compares the price to the competition and it looks like a good value. The buyer makes a purchase. Inside the package you include information about how to get a discount for another fishing lure. To receive the discount the customer enters his name and email address on your website. Once you have the customer's email address, you can send information about other products and specials.

Take the time to create a marketing communications plan. For more help, see "Market-Step Product Plan" in Appendix C.

Getting into Retailers and Distributors

When computers were traditionally sold in retail stores, Dell Computer turned the industry around by selling direct to the customer. The company started out in a college dorm room and grew as an inexpensive alternative to IBM personal computers. Dell first sold to other college students, then in local Texas cities, and then spread nationally through magazine advertising and word of mouth.

New products often get started by marketing directly to customers. As product sales grow, continue to sell direct and add salespeople and/or add distributors and retailers.

While you might want your product sold at Wal-Mart, this is not always the best place to start. Big retailers tend to play with big suppliers who have an established, positive track record. Before approaching the large chain stores, start with small independent stores and small distributors to gain a track record of sales. Distributors and retailers will generally order a small amount for a test. If the product sells, they'll order more.

Retailers come in various forms and include traditional storefronts as well as product catalogs and Internet stores. In general, distributors and retailers look for products that have:

- A large potential sales volume and high margin to generate a profit (e.g., margins can range from 35% to 70% for durable goods, and 10% to 25% for consumables)
- Perceived value to the end-user (e.g., solves a problem or meets a need or want)
- Nice packaging similar to products they currently carry
- The ability to produce the product in the volume they need

Support, in the form of in-store demos, point of sales displays, advertising, and promotion is also a key selection factor. Retailers want support and welcome just about anything you can do to help generate sales, but you'll need to find out their specific desires.

To get started, be prepared to provide prospective retailers and distributors with the following:

- Color brochures of the product and its uses
- Suggested retail price and costs
- Lists of companies that currently sell the product
- Marketing and promotion plans
- Business history
- Authorized contacts in your company
- Samples (though sometimes not requested)

You should have this information ready by the time you make contact. When you do have these materials ready, take the following steps to approach a distributor or retailer:

1. Search the Internet for distributors and retailers that carry your product type. Use a search engine with keywords such as ["your product type" and "retailer"].

2. Call companies and ask to talk with the Buyer or Category Manager who handles your product type. Ask for policies and procedures for carrying new products.
3. Send any material requested. Create a short introductory letter providing a general description and the benefits of your product, along with your background and credentials.
4. Follow-up with a telephone call to make sure they received your package. Then, ask about the next steps.

Keep in mind that most buyers do not have time for presentations. They want to see your marketing materials first, and then decide if they want to talk further.

Your other option is to work with a sales representative who regularly meets with buyers. The sales representative works as an agent on your behalf and is paid on commission. Certain sales representatives have established trusting relationships with buyers. They know what the buyer wants, and the buyer trusts the rep to deliver quality products that will sell. Talk to buyers and ask if they could recommend any reps. Also, use a search engine with keywords ["your product type" and "sales representative"].

Tip: You can approach a retailer as a "second source" of a product. If your product is comparable to a product that a store already carries, they might be interested in a backup supplier. This is a good strategy for you to get started to build a track record of sales. And point out that your product is 100% returnable. Since most retailers suffer losses for products that don't sell, ordering a fully returnable product eliminates their risk.

Fulfillment and Inventory

You have a few options for distributing your product – shipping it yourself, using a fulfillment house, or having the manufacturer ship directly to the customer. Compare costs and time-savings to determine the best method for you.

A fulfillment house will store your product in inventory, take credit card orders, and ship to your customer while charging you a percentage of the sales and often a monthly inventory fee. Since they store inventory and are always available to take orders and ship your product, they're good to use. You can find fulfillment houses by searching the Internet with keywords ["your product type" and "fulfillment"].

Distribution Planning

Use this template to help organize your distribution planning.

- Name the regions that your product type will be sold initially (e.g., just in your area, the coastal regions, mountain areas, state, entire country, world):

- Name the distributors and retailers that will carry your product type (e.g., local stores, regional distributors):

- Uncover the typical margins for your product type (ask distributors and retailers for the normal range):

- Name where inventory will be stored (e.g., your home, fulfillment center, the manufacturer):

- Determine the shipping methods for sending your product out (e.g., regular post, FedEx, UPS, fulfillment center, direct from the manufacturer):

Regulations and Certifications

Your product might require certification or need to conform to certain regulations. If so, make sure to look at this early because certifications and regulations may involve long lead times and expense.

Even if it's not required, certification can provide a competitive advantage and offer peace of mind for potential customers. For example, two power tools are offered for sale. Their prices are about the same and they offer similar features. But one proudly displays a safety certification seal of approval. In this case, buyers will tend to purchase the certified product.

Some certifications are organized within an industry and are not government-based. For example, Microsoft has certification programs that inform customers that certain independent software products conform to Microsoft standards. Microsoft has designated official labs that perform tests for a fee. Once your product passes, you can announce these positive results in a press release and add a certification logo to your product box and website.

Occasionally, customers will require certification before buying your product. For example, a customer was once interested in using my wireless modem to transmit oil-processing data. The catch was that they could only use products certified in hazardous environments. After some research, I discovered that the testing process would cost $10,000 and take two months to complete. In addition, the product would need modifications to pass the test. As a result, I decided it wasn't worth the cost of the certification and modification as compared to product sales.

To uncover certification guidelines for your product type, contact the following certification organizations:

- **UL** – Underwriters Laboratories Inc. (www.ul.com) is an independent, not-for-profit product safety testing and certification organization. They offer services to help companies achieve certification acceptance for their products in the United States whether it's an electrical device, a programmable system, or a company's quality process. A UL mark for an electrical device such as a lamp is not required by law but offers peace of mind to the consumer.
- **CSA** – Canadian Standards Association (www.csa.ca) is a not-for-profit membership-based association serving

business, industry, government, and consumers. They test many products for compliance to national and international standards, and issue the CSA mark. CSA is recognized by the United States Occupational Safety and Health Administration (OSHA) as a "Nationally Recognized Testing Laboratory" for products sold in the United States.

- **CE** – The CE mark (www.cemarking.net) is a mandatory European marking for certain product groups. It indicates conformity with essential health and safety requirements set out in European Directives. The letters "CE" stand for Conformité Européenne, French for "European Conformity." The CE mark must be affixed to products sold in Europe (e.g., medical devices, machinery, industrial installations, toys, electrical equipment, electronics, domestic appliances, pressure equipment, personal protective equipment, recreational craft, refrigerators, etc.). CE marking does not apply to cosmetics, chemicals, pharmaceuticals, and foodstuffs.

For specific guidance, contact a local UL, CSA, or CE test lab listed on their websites or found in the Yellow Pages under Laboratories – Testing.

To get your product certified:

1. Contact a test lab and ask for guidance.
2. Describe your product and ask for a price quote to test your product.
3. Send your product to the lab.
4. The lab performs tests and issues you a report that your product either passed or failed the tests.
5. If your product failed the test, make changes and send a new product to the lab.
6. If a regulating agency oversees your product type, submit a "passed" test report to them. The regulatory agency will review the report and issue a certification.

7. Put the certification mark on your product, packaging, website, brochure, and other communications.

For example, a wireless device in the United States must pass Federal Communications Commission (FCC) testing before use in the public airwaves. A wireless device is sent to an independent test lab to check for harmful emissions. If the device conforms to FCC standards, the lab issues a report saying the product conforms to emission standards. The wireless device and report are then shipped to the FCC to finalize approval. The FCC process can take approximately three months from the time the product is submitted to a lab until final approval.

DEVELOPMENT PLANNING

Product Requirements

Planning for development is one of the keys to success. To get started, you should create a Product Requirements document. A Product Requirements document lists what you want your product to have and do. Product Requirements are written from the customer's perspective. This document helps define the scope, direction, and focus of what you need to develop. Product Requirements along with drawings, diagrams, and photographs provide further clarification to designers and manufacturers. A Product Requirements document will increase your chances that a designer and manufacturer will create the product as you intended, rather than trying to read your mind. This document is simple to create with your wordprocessor and can be as little as one or two pages. Product Requirements includes:

- Features
- Functionality
- Appearance
- Performance levels
- Quality and reliability levels
- User's environment

- Packaging and labeling needs
- Certification and regulation specifications
- Cost levels
- Forecast of units to manufacture
- Timeline for shipment

Review the Prototype Requirements you created in Step Three. Add whatever lessons you learned from the prototype evaluation and any new functionality required to pass regulations and certifications programs. Create Product Requirements with the following steps:

1. List each of the customer's problems, needs, and wants.
2. For each problem, need, and want, make lists of features and functions that provide a solution.
3. Modify and enhance the features and functions based on your innovation, positioning, pricing, quality, style, and product life.
4. Prioritize the list according to features and functions customers are willing buy.
5. Write the list of features and functions into the language of a Product Requirements document such as "The product will have ..." or "The product must perform at the following level ..."
6. Select the highest priority requirements that can be produced quickly and within your budget.
7. Include drawings and diagrams for clarification.

Manufacturing Your Product

Manufacturing involves turning your design into a finished product. While it's possible to manufacture the product yourself, I recommend you outsource production to a contract manufacturer. Outsourcing the manufacturing process will allow you to concentrate on design and marketing. Later, if you decide to manufacture yourself, you'll have learned from the outsourcing experience.

Sample Product Requirements
for a Tabletop Electric Fan

1. The fan will operate at 120 volts, 60 Hz, 0.5 amps.

2. The electric motor will have a life of 10,000 hours.

3. Input voltage regulation will tolerate plus or minus 12 volts.

4. The fan speed is variable at high, medium, and low.

5. High speed will be at 180 revolutions per minute.

6. Medium speed will be at 90 revolutions per minute.

7. Low speed will be at 60 revolutions per minute.

8. There will be four pushbutton switches located on the base and labeled: Off, High, Medium, and Low.

9. There will be a pushbutton switch next to the fan assembly and labeled as Oscillation

10. The fan will oscillate over 90 degrees at a rate of once per ten seconds.

11. The fan will have three blades: each blade 12 inches in diameter and made of ABS white plastic.

12. The blade will be enclosed in a coated aluminum cage.

13. The fan must operate in an environment with temperatures ranging from 32 to 125 degrees Fahrenheit, and humidity from 20% to 100%.

14. The fan must last for at least five years.

15. The fan must pass UL certification.

16. Total parts costs cannot exceed $8.

17. Shipment will begin May 1, 2004.

18. There will be 5,000 fans produced for the first ship date.

19. There will be 5,000 fans produced each month for the following year.

To outsource manufacturing, look for contract manufacturers specializing in your product type. Use a search engine such as Google and keywords ["your product type" and "contract manufacturing"]. Also, look in the Yellow Pages for manufacturers under the following headings:

- Assembly and Fabricating
- Electronic Parts Assemblers
- Manufacturing – Contract
- Plastics Fabricators

Don't be intimidated if you're starting out small. Some manufacturers will work on small production items. Look for advertising messages such as "No job too small" or "Short runs our specialty" or other indicators that a manufacturer will work with inventors and start-up entrepreneurs.

Manufacturers want to see the following to provide a quote to produce your product:

- Drawings and diagrams of each part with exact dimensions and specifications
- Drawings of how parts physically interact (e.g., exploded view diagram, or system flowchart)
- Bill of materials (list of all parts that make up the product)

The general steps a manufacturer will take to produce your product include:

1. Reviewing plans and drawings
2. Ordering parts and materials
3. Designing and setting up an assembly line
4. Performing production of parts and assemblies
5. Performing inspection of parts and assemblies
6. Performing quality acceptance testing
7. Monitoring quality yields and improving processes
8. Packing and shipping the product

Design Engineering

Some manufacturers have engineers on staff to produce drawings and diagrams, but I recommend hiring an engineer on your own. The engineer will act on your behalf as a liaison to the manufacturer to handle technical issues as they may arise. Look in the Yellow Pages for designers and engineers under the following headings:

- Designers – Industrial
- Engineers – Electronic
- Engineers – Mechanical
- Product Designers

Interview engineers and designers to discover if they have experience with your product type. Also check references and credentials. Before discussing your product, ask them to sign your non-disclosure agreement. Provide your Product Requirements and request a price quote to produce drawings and diagrams. If need be, ask if they'll interact with a manufacturer and work with you as the product is being produced.

Tip: While still in the planning stage, design your product with manufacturing in mind. This means simplifying the design by using the fewest number of parts and as many similar parts as possible. For example, if your product uses screws, have all screws the same type and the same size. This seems obvious, but products exist that use a mix of Philips and slot screws. Since parts are purchased in quantity, you'll save money by using as many similar parts as possible. Also, the lower the number of parts often leads to less expensive assembly costs. Another way to reduce costs is by designing parts that snap or screw together during assembly rather than needing fasteners or tools.

Manufacturing Software Products

Manufacturing for a software or music product is much easier than a physical product. It's simply a matter of disk duplication.

You can outsource duplication or do this yourself with one or more CD burners. Some disk duplication companies offer additional services such as printing and packaging. Compare prices of these additional services to companies that produce packaging separately. See Chapter 16 for more details about packaging.

Project Plan

A project plan is a list of activities and timeline of your entire product development. Creating a project plan will help provide clarity, flesh out assumptions, and uncover technical and practical details. In addition, project plans generally lead to faster project completion, greater product quality, and a closer alignment of product functionality to customer needs.

Your project plan does not have to be elaborate. The methods I suggest will allow you to create a project that's streamlined and simple. A few pages may suffice depending on the complexity of the product.

Keep in mind that if you intend to outsource product development, all aspects of the product should be described so that the designer has optimal clarity to complete tasks. Create a project plan with the following outline:

- Product Description
- Goals and Objectives
- Possible Issues
- Deadlines
- Tasks

Tasks make up the bulk of a project plan. For your project plan, create a list of tasks with the following guidelines:

1. **Identify activities** – Visualize, brainstorm, and perform research to determine all possible major and minor development activities for completing the product. Talk to people who have created your product type before,

reverse engineer similar products, review patents, and talk with designers, engineers, and product consultants.

2. **Identify tasks** – For each major and minor activity, list the individual tasks to complete them.

3. **Group similar tasks together** – To speed up development time, look for groups of tasks that can be performed at the same time or by the same person.

4. **Order tasks** – Some tasks will need to be completed before others. Order tasks within each group.

5. **Estimate time to complete** – Estimate the time to perform each task in terms of days, weeks, or months. It's just an estimate, so don't worry if you're off by a few days here and there.

6. **Determine total time** – Summarize time needed to complete the entire project. Keep in mind that some tasks cannot be started until a previous task is completed. To shorten project time, look for tasks that can be worked on in tandem.

7. **Find resources** – If you're working on the project with others, assign people or companies to each task. Note that more people doesn't always guarantee shorter project time. Microsoft's Bill Gates has been known to understaff projects to create an entrepreneurial atmosphere and minimize costs.

Another way to get started with a project plan is to flow-chart key activities. First visualize the entire process. Then, with a piece of paper, draw activities and see what items come first, next, and which are missing.

In the project plan example on the next page, a list of tasks and timelines are shown. Tasks are grouped by Product Planning, Manufacturing, Product Artwork, Packaging, User Documentation, and Distribution.

Note that in the Time column, "d" represents days and "w" represents weeks. Also, Time in this example is for work performed during weekdays and not over weekends.

Sample Project Plan			
TASK	Start	Time	Finish
PRODUCT PLANNING			
Create product requirements and manufacturing plans	Jun 1	10d	Jun 14
Present Product Requirements to engineer and manufacturer	Jun 15	1d	Jun 15
Engineer to provide up to three CAD prototypes	Jun 16	10d	Jun 29
Approve one prototype	Jun 30	1d	Jun 30
Engineer works on detailed design	Jul 1	2w	Jul 17
Approve final design	Jul 18	1d	Jul 18
Engineer creates test requirements	Jul 20	6d	Jul 27
MANUFACTURING			
Manufacturer runs production	Jul 28	2w	Aug 10
Product ships to distribution center	Aug 11	3d	Aug 15
PRODUCT ARTWORK			
Artist to create product artwork	Jul 6	1w	Jul 14
PACKAGING			
Packaging requirements planning	Jun 30	8d	Jul 11
Packaging company creates a prototype and cost estimates	Jul 12	1w	Jul 18
Approve one package prototype	Jul 19	1d	Jul 19
Artist to create packaging artwork	Jul 20	5d	Jul 26
Packaging company runs production	Jul 27	5d	Aug 2
Packaging company ships packaging to product manufacturer	Aug 3	1d	Aug 3
USER DOCUMENTATION			
User Manual first draft	Jul 3	2w	Jul 14
User Manual photo shots	Jul 17	1d	Jul 17
User Manual edits	Jul 18	3d	Jul 20
User Manual final review	Jul 21	3d	Jul 25
User Manual formatting	Jul 26	5d	Aug 1
User Manual printing and shipment	Aug 2	1w	Aug 8
DISTRIBUTION			
Receive product and packaging	Aug 16	2d	Aug 17
Product Availability	Aug 18	1d	Aug 18

I recommend using Microsoft Project to organize and track your project. It allows you to list each task, set a start date, estimate duration, set task precedence, and assign resources. The application will automatically generate Gantt charts, PERT diagrams, and more as needed.

A Gantt chart is a graphic display of tasks that will help you see the relationships and timelines of all the tasks. A Project Evaluation and Review Technique (PERT) chart is another graphics method to help organize tasks. Check the Microsoft website for more information on Microsoft Project. Overall, create a project plan with whichever method is easiest for you to organize tasks and monitor progress.

Launch Checklist

A Launch Checklist is another handy tool for staying organized and on track. The term "launch" means that the product is produced, available for shipping, and you're ready to receive sales orders. The launch date is often called first customer ship (FCS) or general availability (GA). The launch checklist is an overview of all the tasks that need completion before introducing your product in the market.

Visualize your product being shipped out the door to the customer, and then think about all the pieces that produce product sales. You'll include every item you'll need to accomplish before launch. This launch checklist will keep you focused and free your mind to work creatively.

Some items such as advertising can have long lead times. For example, if you want an advertisement to appear in a magazine at the same time you launch your product, you might have to submit your ad materials three months before launch date. Review the lead times for each task to make sure they'll be ready for the launch.

Sample Product Launch Checklist

When the following items are completed, the product is ready to launch.

Product
- ❑ The product is designed
- ❑ The product receives industry certification
- ❑ The product is produced
- ❑ The product passes testing
- ❑ Packaging and shipping containers are completed and received

Documentation
- ❑ User manual is written and edited
- ❑ Online help is tested and verified

Marketing
- ❑ Beta product is sent to product review magazines (at least two months before launch)
- ❑ Advertising will appear by launch date (place at least three months before launch)
- ❑ Brochures are produced (printed and electronic files)
- ❑ Direct mailers are designed, mailing list selected (printed)
- ❑ Press Release is written and contacts identified (send on launch date – submit by email)
- ❑ Product Launch Kit is written (electronic files)
- ❑ Website contains product information, contact information, a sales lead form, and press release
- ❑ A product launch party is scheduled

Sales and Support
- ❑ Distributor agreements are in place
- ❑ Sales and customer service people are trained
- ❑ Customer relationship database is ready
- ❑ Sales letter is written and edited
- ❑ The 800 telephone number is operational

Post-Launch
- ❑ Track sales leads (amount and source)
- ❑ Track sales revenue (amount and source)

Budget Setting

We only have a certain amount of money to spend on development, marketing, and sales. How will we spend it? Different product types, different competitive environments, and various stages of growth in the market will dictate the amount of money you'll need and how it should be allocated.

For a budget example, cell phones are highly technical, very competitive, and the market is still growing. As a result, development and advertising costs are high. In contrast, standard flashlights have been around a long time and have a mature market. Therefore, development costs are minimal and the budget emphasis is on retail packaging.

The following is a guideline for allocating money from initial idea to product launch. For example, let's say you have $10,000 to spend. Using the given allocation percentages, you would plan to spend $1,000 (10%) on market research, $6,000 (60%) on product development, $500 (5%) on packaging, and $2,500 (25%) on marketing communications.

Budget Allocation Guideline	
Product Area	**Allocation**
Market Research	10%
Development and Production	60%
Packaging	5%
Marketing Communications	25%

On the other hand, if you plan to raise money, investors want to know how much you'll need. To determine the amount, you'll review your project plan, assigning a dollar amount to each task in terms of the cost of labor, overhead, and materials. For typical financial allocations used in your product industry, examine the book *Industry Norms & Key Business Ratios* by Dun & Bradstreet. You'll find ratios of assets, liabilities, sales, and profit broken down by industry. You can usually find this book in the reference or social science section of a public or university library. I also recommend discussing development and marketing costs with an accountant experienced with your product type.

Your Budget
How much money can you budget to develop and market your product? $_____.   Allocate this amount across the following product areas.

Product Area	Allocation %	Amount $
Market Research		
Development and Production		
Packaging		
Marketing Communications		

Excellent! You have completed Step Four. Now, take these plans and turn them into real product development and marketing programs by following the strategies in the next chapter.

In addition to product planning, it's time to start thinking about setting up a business entity. For more information, see "Funding Your Idea" in Appendix E, and "Business Startup" in Appendix F.

Chapter 16
Step Five – Develop It

If the automobile had followed the same development cycle as the computer, a Rolls-Royce would today cost $100, get one million miles to the gallon, and explode once a year, killing everyone inside.

Robert X. Cringely

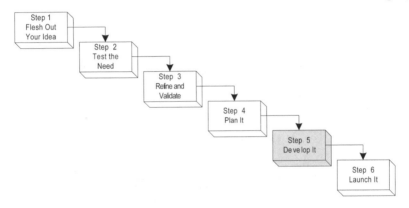

The fifth step of the **Market-Step** process is development. Your product comes to life in stages. It started as a concept in your mind. Then, it came into form as a prototype. In the development stage, it continues to grow as an alpha product, beta product, and then the first commercially available product. In Step Five you'll:

Develop the Product
1. Convert requirements into specifications
2. Create a bill of materials
3. Write a test plan
4. Write user documentation
5. Initiate production

Beta Test
6. Plan a beta test
7. Recruit beta testers
8. Distribute to beta testers
9. Obtain beta feedback

Develop Marketing Programs
10. Develop a marketing brand and theme
11. Select a product name
12. Create packaging

If you're completing Step Five by yourself, complete activities one through twelve in order. If you have two or more people, you may save time by working in tandem. A person or team can develop the product, while another person or team can conduct the beta test, and others can develop marketing programs.

PRODUCT DEVELOPMENT

If you're skilled in design and manufacturing, great. If not, use the information here to guide your work with designers, engineers, and contract manufacturers.

Convert Requirements into Specifications

The first development step is to convert product requirements into specifications. In Step Four you created a Product Requirements document. Now, you'll need to examine each requirement and create specifications. Specifications are the details of each feature and function of your product. If you hire an engineer, ask him or her to create specifications for you.

Step Five – Development Flowchart

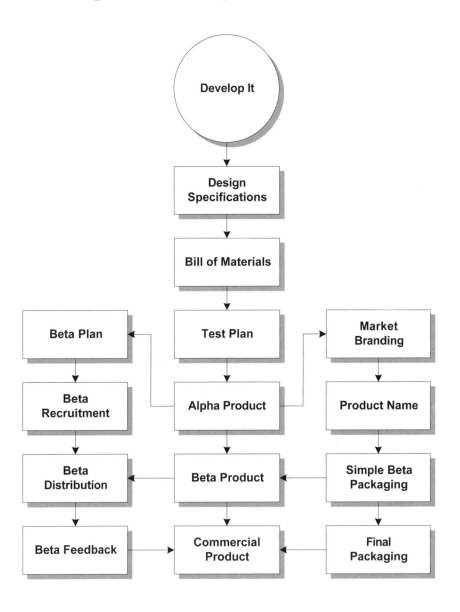

Your specifications may include details about:

- Capacity
- Color
- Energy: Voltage, Current, Power
- Environment: Temperature, Humidity, Pressure
- Function
- Input, Output
- Materials
- Movement: Direction, Speed, Rate
- Reliability, Stress, Strain
- Resolution
- Shape
- Size: Length, Width, Height, Area, Diameter
- Time
- Tolerance
- Weight

In addition to specifying component characteristics, specifications can include details for accepted standards. For example, the product requirements state: "This product will operate in compliance to IEEE 802.11 standards." And so, the specification will outline the details of IEEE 802.11. Standards for software, electronics, clothing, food, etc., are maintained by independent organizations and the government. Standards exist for safety and/or to allow easier integration of parts and systems. See if there are standards that exist for your product type. You'll find more information about standards at the National Institute of Standards (www.nist.gov), and the International Organization for Standardization (www.iso.org).

Not only must you consider the specifications of each component, but also you must specify how components interact. For example, a motor interacts with a circuit board via a cable and connectors. In this case, you'll need to specify the cable length, number of leads, material, voltage levels, etc. Some mechanical products have gears that mesh, so you'd need to specify how two gears interact in terms of angle, number of teeth that mesh, lubrication needed, and the like.

Specifications – Components

Create specifications for each component of your product, using this template as a guide.

Component Name: _____.
List specifications that apply to this component:

Component Name: _____.
List specifications that apply to this component:

Component Name: _____.
List specifications that apply to this component:

Specifications – Interface

Create specifications for the components' interface, using this template as a guide.

Component Names: _____ | _____.
List specifications that apply to the interface between these components:

Component Names: _____ | _____.
List specifications that apply to the interface between these components:

Component Names: _____ | _____.
List specifications that apply to the interface between these components:

Make or Buy

Instead of developing new components for your product, purchase as many as possible. The decision to make or buy comes down to time and budget. If components are hard to get or more expensive than producing yourself, you might have to create them yourself.

If you buy a component, you can use it as is, or modify it to suit the overall design of your product. As noted in the following development diagram, it's possible that your product will include some components you design as well as those you buy.

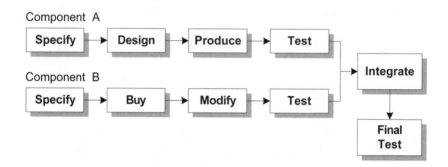

Let's use the tabletop electric fan as an example. For each component, we'll determine whether to make or buy it:

- **Fan blade** – Innovative cooling properties, derived from a unique blade design, constitute a major selling point of this fan. You've specified the dimensions, curvature, flexibility, durability, and materials of the blade, then search parts catalogs to discover nothing like it exists. Therefore, you'll need to design and produce it yourself.
- **Fan cover** – The fan cover is an important safety component. You search catalogs and find many types of covers already exist that might work with your design. You call manufacturers to receive a few samples to test.
- **Motor** – The electric motor has been around for years and is now a standard item. You search and find a reliable brand conforming to your specifications.

- **Electrical controls and pushbutton switches** – You specify that you'll need a circuit to control the variable high, medium, and low speeds. The electronic parts are standard and readily available. You hire an electrical engineer to design a circuit board.
- **Fan Housing** – The fan housing is specific to your innovation and therefore you will have to design it yourself. You give the requirements and specifications to an industrial designer who creates a computer-aided design.

Bill of Materials

Manufacturers want to know all of the parts that make up your product and packaging. A standard method of tracking parts is known as a Bill of Materials. A bill of materials is often abbreviated as BOM and pronounced like "bomb." You'll need to provide a simple bill of materials to get a price quote from a manufacturer. If you're hiring an engineer, ask him or her to create a BOM for you. When production begins, your engineer or manufacturer will create a complete BOM with a list of product components and its parts, drawings, documentation, packaging, and shipping material. The following is a sample bill of materials.

Bill of Materials				
ID	Level	Description	Qty	Part Number
1	1	Brass plate	1	XYZ 67-89-01
2	2	Philips bolt 3" brass	4	XYZ 123-4567
3	2	Hex Nuts #2 brass	4	XYZ 123-8901
4	2	Washers #2 brass	4	XYZ 123-2345

A typical BOM has sequential ID numbers, level numbers indicating assemblies and corresponding sub-assemblies, part description, quantity, and part number. Purchased parts will come with a part number. If you're designing the part yourself, create a part number using a simple scheme. Always check with the manufacturer first to find out their preferred format. Create a bill of materials using a wordprocessor, spreadsheet, or material requirements planning software.

Test Cases

Testing validates design. You're checking to make sure components and the whole product conform to your requirements, specifications, and regulations. How to test a circuit board, software code, or mechanical parts is outside the scope of this book. But, in general, a test plan is written to include specific test cases that examine every aspect of your product.

Test cases exercise the entire product and its components under varying conditions for non-conformance. If you're not skilled at developing test plans, hire a test lab, test engineer, or quality assurance person to write a test plan. If you use a contract manufacturer, test plans are given to the manufacturer to execute as the product is being produced. On the other hand, you can provide product requirements and specifications to the manufacturer who will develop test plans for you. Check with the manufacturer about the cost of this service.

For testing assistance, look in the Yellow Pages under Test Lab or Quality Assurance. Also search the Internet for organizations that have local chapters whose members you may contact. Quality organizations include:

- American Society for Quality
  (www.asq.org)
- Association for Quality and Participation
  (www.aqp.org)
- Association for Manufacturing Excellence
  (www.ame.org)
- Society for Software Quality
  (www.ssq.org)

User Documentation

Your customers will need instructions about installing, setting up, and using your product. Good documentation often creates a competitive advantage. Types of documentation include step-by-step installation guides, user manuals, reference guides, and online help. Since clear and concise documentation is important, seek the advice of a technical writer. Search the Internet for technical writers or the Yellow Pages under Writing Services or Technical Manual Preparation.

Before contacting a writer, prepare a description of your needs. When interviewing writers, your ability to work comfortably with them is as important as their experience with your product type. Once you hire someone, ask the writer to create a style guide to ensure consistency of all your documentation. Then, provide as much content for each document as possible and let the writer edit and fill in the gaps.

To keep product costs low, print as little documentation as possible. Your customers will need basic instructions to get started. But detailed documentation could be made available on a CD or as a download from the Internet.

Product Production

A product such as the tabletop electric fan has several different components and materials. There's the plastic fan blade and housing, the metal blade cover, motor, and electrical circuit. In this case, you'd want a manufacturer who can produce the plastics, metals, and circuits. Some manufacturers perform all of these in-house and some will sub-contract to specialty manufacturers. For example, a manufacturer who produces only electronic circuits will outsource plastics and metal fabrication. The plastics and metal parts are produced and delivered to the primary manufacturer who integrates them with the electrical controls. In this scenario, you only have to deal with the primary manufacturer, who coordinates separate component production behind the scenes. Before approaching a manufacturer:

- Review the accuracy of your product requirements, specifications, and project plan.
- Create lists, drawings, diagrams, and flowcharts that provide details of the product features and functions.
- Create a bill of materials of all the parts that are used in the beta product.
- Determine production quantities in terms of an alpha, beta, and full production over the first year. Quantities for an alpha might be as few as five, while twenty to fifty units for beta.

To get your product manufactured, use the following steps:

1. Search for manufacturers who produce your product type. Talk to a sales representative about getting a product manufactured. Ask for references and whether they're manufacturing for one of your competitors. If so, ask how will they keep your product confidential.
2. Tour manufacturers and look at cleanliness, organization, and quality control.
3. Request a price quote by providing requirements, drawings (paper or computer), bill of materials, production volume, and deadlines.
4. Review quotes for more than just the lowest price. Consider the timeline, ease of working with the manufacturer, and reputation. Ask for detailed explanations of any quote that seems questionable.
5. When you've chosen the manufacturer, they'll probably ask you to sign the quote to indicate acceptance. In addition, they'll also request a deposit.
6. Supply any updated designs or artwork to the manufacturer.
7. The manufacturer will begin planning and ordering parts with quantities suitable for an alpha, beta, and final product.

8. At the same time, begin working on your packaging (explained at the end of this chapter). When packaging is complete, have it shipped to the product manufacturer.

9. When all materials are in place, the manufacturer will begin production. Parts are assembled, tested, and placed into the packaging.

10. As the first products are coming off the production line, be there to monitor, inspect and to make sure the product conforms to your requirements. Look for parts out of alignment, cracks, incorrectly printed artwork, and overall proper function.

Manufacturing Notes and Tips

As you work with a product manufacturer, remember:

- Manufacturing timelines will vary according to the complexity of your product, and the workload and capacity of the manufacturer.
- Typically, manufacturers will not start production until they have all parts and packaging for the initial run in their inventory.
- You can request certain parts to come from a particular vendor, or allow the manufacturer to use their vendor of choice. Compare product quality and cost.
- Manufacturers prefer to run a production line continuously until the volume specified in your contract is completed. If they start and then stop for a period of time, there are setup charges to retool the line.
- For testing, you can provide test instructions and equipment or allow the manufacturer to do it. You'll be charged for parts and labor if the manufacturer has to build special test equipment.
- Provide any products or parts that interact with your product for testing. For example, if you're producing candleholders, provide the manufacturer with the matching candles.

BETA TEST YOUR PRODUCT

A beta test involves trying out your nearly completed product in real situations by representative customers. The beta product has many of the final product's features and functions but lacks finishing touches. A beta test helps uncover any design flaws before final production, and is a final verification that your product meets your customer's needs.

A beta test program can last from one month to many months depending on your product's complexity and the amount of feedback you want. To determine duration, think about how much time it would take you to fully evaluate your product, then multiply that amount by three to five times! The beta process will take longer than you anticipate.

In order to clarify the process to the beta testers, you need to create a beta test agreement for them to sign. This agreement will include non-disclosure of confidential information, liability limits, product limitations, feedback requirements, duration, and any incentives you offer.

The agreement informs beta testers that they are not to discuss the beta test with anyone and not post public messages on the Internet. You must also state that bugs, defects, and errors may occur and that you are not to be held responsible. Ask an attorney to create a beta test agreement. If your budget precludes using an attorney, there are beta test agreements on the Internet that may be of some use. But, I advise you to consult with an attorney for legal advice. The steps to conduct a beta test are:

1. Create a beta test plan
2. Create a beta test agreement
3. Design the beta product with the key features and functions you want to test
4. Recruit beta candidates
5. Send qualified candidates a beta site agreement
6. Produce your beta product
7. Distribute your beta product

8. Call or email beta customers at the outset to encourage product usage
9. Call or email beta customers weekly with prepared questions to gather feedback
10. At the conclusion, send beta customers a thank-you letter and ask them to fill out a final survey
11. Summarize all feedback
12. Make adjustments to your product as needed

To start, I suggest creating a beta test plan that outlines your goals, objectives, timeline, recruitment, and questions you want answered. Create a beta test plan using the sample on the next page as a guide.

Beta Recruitment

You'll need to recruit beta testers as early as possible. Be prepared to spend at least a month to find and recruit candidates. Try recruiting those who already participated in the concept surveys, interviews, and focus groups. In addition, look for new people who are in your target market.

As an incentive to participate in beta testing, you can give the commercially available product away for free or at a discount.

Request a certain number of hours per week or month participation over the length of the beta program. Make sure you get a firm commitment to provide feedback in exchange for the incentives you provide.

Beta Feedback

Regular feedback from your beta customers is crucial. Be prepared to ask specific questions related to installation, usage, clarity of the documentation, and how well the product solves a problem or satisfies a need. You can direct beta testers to fill out a feedback form on your website, or call to discuss the details.

Sample Beta Test Plan

Goals and Objectives
- Gather feedback on product features and functions
- Test the product in diverse user situations
- Gather testimonials

Program Information
- Start date: 5/1/2003
- Duration: 6 weeks
- Quantity: 25 beta sites

Beta Customer Qualification
- Type of user: Middle income, professional
- Experience level: Uses this type of product daily
- Location of beta site: Continental U.S.

Beta Recruitment
- Contact people who completed a concept survey
- Contact people who attended the focus group
- Send a recruitment email to target market list

Beta Feedback Questions
- Was the product easy to install?
- Was the product easy to use?
- How well did the product solve your problem or meet your needs?
- What feature was the most important?
- How was the quality of the user documentation?
- What is your overall assessment of the product?
- Would you recommend this product to someone else?
- What are your comments and suggestions?

Product Package
- Shipping box
- Product
- Cover letter
- Installation instructions and quick start document
- Problem report form

From Beta to Final Development

When your beta test is complete, send a thank-you letter, and ask participants to fill out a survey to summarize their feedback. You'll need to review the beta test results to decide which features and functions, if any, need to be modified before you launch your commercial product. A change might mean modifying designs, test plans, and documentation. Changes might also mean a slip in your production and shipment schedule.

While you'll want to ship the product as early as possible, it's best to fix any key saleable features and issues that affect overall quality. Go through the entire cycle of design, production, and testing if need be. A product is ready for release when it performs as specified. You may exclude new features that are just nice to have and not key saleable features, from the current version. They can be added to later versions.

How many of your products should you manufacture? The answer depends in part on your budget and in part on your risk tolerance. Beta test results will reveal customer enthusiasm. Talk to distributors and retailers to find out how many products of your type are selling. Remember that retailers will often start out stocking a small trial amount. As an estimate of the number of products to manufacture, think about the number of buyers you can reach and the percentage of those interested.

MARKETING DEVELOPMENT

You'll need to think about marketing during the development stage of creating your product. Otherwise, the completed product just sits while you come up with marketing programs and materials. Marketing and product development are interrelated. If you are developing with a team or outside consultants, the product and marketing should be worked on in tandem. If it's just you, you'll need to divide your time. For some of my projects, I designate certain days for marketing and other days for development. For example, Thursday and Friday may be for marketing such as creating sales and promotions, while the other days I'm in development mode. This method will allow you to stay focused and develop the entire product in a balanced and integrated manner.

Branding Your Product

Branding is a messaging technique that instills a positive emotional reaction when people think about your product. Branding distinguishes your product from the competition. Branding also builds familiarity that breeds loyalty, and then purchasing preference. For example, the Coca-Cola logo prompts many people to think about having fun as well as having a refreshing beverage. This impression is reinforced by advertising showing people partying and having fun while drinking Coca-Cola.

We identify a brand by a variety of elements such as its product name, logo, images, colors, fonts, sounds (e.g., song, chimes, distinctive motorcycle engine), symbols, shapes, slogans, word choice (e.g., sophisticated, slang, folksy, earthy), and/or user experience.

There are bottles of water and then there's Perrier. Yes, Perrier is just sparkling water but it was branded to confer sophistication and class. The Chevy truck was just another truck until General Motors started using the song "Like a Rock" by Bob Seger in TV and radio advertising. They also repeated the tagline "Like a Rock" in print advertising. Chevy trucks soon soared to number one in sales.

The key to effective branding is using consistent and repetitive marketing messages in advertising, brochures, packaging, promotional items, trade show signage, website, and customer service. The messaging must convey something customers can relate to so that they think your product is a reflection of themselves. In essence, branding communicates a promise that your product will lead to fame, fortune, recognition, romance, safety, and other motivators.

Do all products need branding? Not necessarily. Many people are motivated primarily by low price. So, if your strategy is to cater to this market segment, and you want to keep your costs to a minimum, branding is not a major issue. Nor would branding be an issue if you were selling private-label products with a retail store brand name.

Product Naming

You should select a product name by the time you start beta testing. Selecting a product name does not have to be difficult. Look at your list of product benefits and positioning as a guide. Names like DieHard for a battery and Close-Up for a toothpaste are good examples of the product benefit within the name. Other examples of combining words into names include the Hewlett-Packard LaserJet and Adobe PageMaker. Another way to create a name is to combine and fuse words together such as Eveready and Velcro (velvet and crochet). Start with your product's benefits and brainstorm from there.

Use a name that's easy to pronounce and spell. Use a search engine such as Google or AltaVista with your product name as the keyword to see if the product name is taken. Also, go to the USPTO website and search the trademark database for names.

Marketing Theme

To evoke branding you need to start by creating a theme. Your theme must be tied to your product positioning and centered on whatever your customers are seeking.

Notice that positioning a product as expensive and/or high quality, often involves a theme of richness. For example, the mustard Grey Poupon has been positioned as a premium product. The theme involved a Rolls Royce limousine as a luxury icon. The idea is that by tasting Grey Poupon, you would feel as if you are experiencing luxury.

The San Jose Sharks of the National Hockey League have the theme of a snarling shark with black and teal colors. Their market research revealed that women prefer teal, and men prefer black. The Sharks made their logo, team jersey, and website follow this theme. Interestingly, even when the team had played poorly, their merchandise sales were among the best in sports.

Marketing Theme

Brainstorm the theme, look, and feel of your marketing communications program.

Overall Theme
Think of a few different themes that might appeal to your audience (e.g., the look, setting, the story you want to tell):

Images
Brainstorm the type of images that accentuate the theme (e.g., photos, drawings, graphics, color combinations):

Headlines
Make a list of possible headlines (an effective headline often includes a statement of benefits or the asking of a question; look at other products and see what grabs your attention as a starting point):

Sub-headlines / Slogans
Brainstorm possible sub-headlines or slogans that are catchy and memorable (e.g., The milk chocolate melts in your mouth, not in your hand; Got Milk?; Where's the Beef?). Creating a slogan is not easy, but think of your positioning and then Just Do It:

Body – Key benefit points
Take your key benefits and advantages that improve the customer's life and make a list of phrases to use in all your messages (e.g., The best method to generate more sales):

Body – Key copy points
List key messages you want to get across (e.g., unique product features, a special reputation, or a limited opportunity):

Your marketing communications can be based on the following themes:

- Animals
- Architecture
- Family life
- Farming
- Flowers
- Fun, friends, and parties
- Historic events, people, periods
- Luxury
- Mountains
- Oceans
- Sports
- Sun and stars
- Technology
- Travel and world geography

Packaging Your Product

Packaging can be as important as the product itself. This is especially true for retail products. Shoppers often make assumptions and purchase decisions based on the packaging. It's just human nature and there's no way around it. Packaging serves four key objectives:

- Containing and protecting the product
- Preventing theft
- Getting attention, persuading, and informing
- Positioning the product to reflect price, quality, and convenience

Your first packaging consideration should be product distribution. If you're selling retail, the package must have an outstanding shelf presence. The package must command attention to lure a shopper browsing products. Before designing your packaging, talk to retailers about their requirements such as format, size, and weight. On the other hand, if you're selling business to business or shipping direct to the customer, packaging flair is less important. Still, packaging quality must match the quality and price level of the product. For example, you would not wrap an expensive Rolex watch in a paper bag.

Packaging comes in layers (e.g., product container, outer package, and shipping box). For example, Kodak film and its metal cartridge is the product. The plastic tube is the product container. The yellow box they're packed into is the outer package. And there's a shipping box, also known as the master carton, that's used to ship a quantity of product to the retail store or distributor. Product packaging consists of:

- A product container (e.g., a bottle, cardboard box, plastic case).
- Outer packaging to hold the product and provide information.
- Material inside the packaging to protect and hold the product in place (e.g., cardboard, foam, plastic).
- Information printed on the package or label may include product name, company name, logo, sales copy, instructions, warnings, list of product components or ingredients, testimonials, awards, location made, price, and UPC.
- A master carton holding and protecting a quantity of the product.
- Information printed on the shipping container (e.g., company name, product name, product quantity, weight, and handling instructions).

UPC Barcode

Retail packages use the industry standard Universal Product Code (UPC) barcode. The UPC consists of twelve characters representing the product manufacturer, product, and a check digit. The Uniform Code Council, Inc., a non-profit standards organization, manages UPC.

To create a UPC bar code, you have to become a member of the Uniform Code Council (www.uc-council.com). To become a member you need to fill out an application online. There are many questions you'll need to answer, such as product type and annual revenue, before they'll provide a UPC. Expect to pay an initial fee of $750 and up for a block of 100 UPCs, and then a $150 per year renewal fee. After you sign up, you're assigned an identification number licensed for your company's use. You'll use this number to create your own UPC.

Once you're assigned a UPC number, add a barcode to the packaging artwork. Some graphic design software applications can create barcodes. If not, you can visit a barcode-generating website. For a small fee ($10 to $30) you enter the code on the website and a barcode graphic file is displayed or emailed to you. Send the barcode graphic file to the graphic designer.

Many websites are available to generate barcodes. Use a search engine to find them. I've successfully used Bar Code Graphics, Inc. (www.barcode-graphics.com).

If your product is a book, you do not need a UPC, but you'll need to acquire an International Standard Book Number (ISBN) from RR Bowker (www.bowker.com). ISBNs are issued as a minimum of ten numbers in a block. The fee is currently $225. For more information, go to the ISBN website (www.isbn.org).

I suggest testing the barcode before you finalize the packaging. Take a printout of the barcode to a retail store. Ask if they can do a quick scan for you. If it works, the computer screen connected to the scanner will show the barcode's numbers. If it's not readable, the print quality of the barcode may not be suitable or the code is incorrect.

Master Carton

You'll need a shipping box to send your product to the end-user, retailer, or distributor. Often called a master carton, the shipping box protects the product and packaging. To save money, use a standard cardboard box from an office supply or packing materials company. If your product does not fit a standard box, ask your packaging manufacturer to provide a quote for a shipping container.

The box must be sturdy enough to handle shipping abuses. Both UPS and FedEx have packaging guidelines. Even if you do

---

Packaging Elements

The following are components in packaging. Check off the elements used for your product type (✓).

Product Container
- ❑ Cardboard box
- ❑ Glass bottle
- ❑ Metal can
- ❑ Plastic bottle, box, or case

Outer Package Material
- ❑ Cardboard
- ❑ Glass
- ❑ Metal
- ❑ Plastic

Outer Package Design
- ❑ Company information
- ❑ Product description
- ❑ Expiration date
- ❑ Graphics
- ❑ Industry certifications
- ❑ Instructions
- ❑ Legal disclaimers
- ❑ Logo
- ❑ Part and/or Serial number
- ❑ Product awards
- ❑ Sales promotion
- ❑ Testimonials
- ❑ UPC barcode
- ❑ Warnings
- ❑ Warranty

Outer Package Type
- ❑ Bag
- ❑ Blister pack (plastic housing over cardboard)
- ❑ Box or Carton
- ❑ Clamshell (two plastic halves folded together)
- ❑ Shrink-wrap

Interior Material
- ❑ Cardboard
- ❑ Foam
- ❑ Plastic

Interior Contents
- ❑ Accessories
- ❑ Coupon / Rebates
- ❑ Instruction guide
- ❑ Promotional materials
- ❑ Registration card
- ❑ User manual
- ❑ Warranty card

Package Placement
- ❑ Hang from a rack
- ❑ Inside a vending machine
- ❑ Ship direct to customer
- ❑ Sit on a shelf or counter

not use them, their websites provide useful guidelines on shipping materials and proper packaging suggestions.

As a simple test, wrap your product in its package and put it the shipping container. Drop the container on a hard surface from a height of four feet. Do it repeatedly and then open the container to see how the product and package survived.

When the sales volume is high enough, you'll ship products by the pallet. A standard pallet is 40 by 48 inches. Therefore, your shipping containers must be able to be stacked evenly on a pallet and sturdy enough to withstand stacking.

You'll also need to have your company name, product UPC barcode, and destination information on the shipping container. I suggest creating a professional-looking label to apply to the box. You can also use a packing slip that folds inside a clear cover with its destination address facing out. Do not list the product on the master container itself. If the product is perceived as valuable, it might attract theft. Also, if you're shipping your product outside the country, check with Customs officials for specific guidelines.

Steps to Create Packaging

Package design should be consistent with your other marketing materials and follow the same branding guidelines. Everything your customer sees should have the same look and feel in terms of images, fonts, style, color, and message.

You can save a lot of money on package design if you use standard items such as a box, bottle, can, bag, tag, or other materials. Otherwise you'll pay extra for setup charges and other costs for custom packaging. And the timeline to create new packaging can easily take four weeks or longer. To create a product package, use the following steps as a guide:

1. Review packaging of similar products and list the elements of the package. Note which elements appear attractive and which do not.

2. Make of list of packaging requirements and sketch possible designs.

3. Contact packaging vendors and discuss your project. Look in the Yellow Pages for Packaging or Package Design and Development headings. Also look for contract packagers on the Packaging Digest website (www.packagingdigest.com) and the Contract Manufacturing and Packaging Association website (www.contractpackaging.org). In general, it's best to find a local company or one with a local sales representative, so you can meet in person. Also, a packaging company located near your product manufacturer will reduce your shipping costs.

4. Discuss your needs and provide a product prototype and other materials that go into the package with the packaging manufacturer.

5. Discuss packaging requirements with distributors, retailers, and shipping companies. Ask retailers how and where your product type is typically displayed.

6. Ask packaging vendors to provide packaging samples to see if they're what you have in mind.

7. Request a price quote based on your forecasted quantity and budget.

8. Contact a graphic designer experienced with product packaging to create the look and layout. Discuss your packaging needs and product positioning. Get a dieline (template) from the packaging vendor to help with the design layout.

9. Develop packaging content such as sales messages, product information, and testimonials for the graphic designer.

10. For retail products, take mock-ups to a retail store to see if your packaging stands out.

11. Approve the final design, and have the graphic designer send artwork to the packaging manufacturer.

12. Review packaging to make sure they're made to your specifications.

13. Ask the packaging vendor to ship finished materials to your product manufacturer.

Tips to consider for your packaging:

- Create a theme with colors and pictures that take product positioning into account. If you want your product to be perceived as festive, then use bright colors and images of people having fun.
- Emphasize the benefits of using your product with messages and images that communicate money, time, safety, a better life, productivity, etc.
- If you have a unique product, use packaging to emphasize its uniqueness. Use a unique shape, material, or images. If your product is sold by retailers, check to make sure they'll accept odd shapes or materials.
- Design the package with the lighting in mind. Will the package be seen in fluorescent, incandescent, or outdoor lighting? Colors are affected by different lighting and may not appear as you intended.
- Artwork can be printed directly on the package or on a label that is affixed to the package.
- Provide instructions on the outside about opening the package. Make your product easy to unpack and repack.
- Ask the retailer about the display method (e.g., hang from a rack, sit on a shelf or counter).
- Take your retail packaging mock-up and put it on a shelf with similar product types to see if it stands out.
- Make your package easy to carry and transport (e.g., bulky packages might need handles).
- Look into recycled and biodegradable materials, especially if your target audience is environmentally conscious.
- If you intend to export your product, review specific country issues such as packaging, advertising, transportation, cultural habits, and legislation.

- Seek feedback from potential customers such as those who beta test your product.
- Familiarize yourself with the Federal Trade Commission's advertising and packaging guidelines. Search for "Fair Packaging and Labeling Act" for the latest information (www.ftc.gov).

Package Design

To help plan your packaging, use this template as a guide.

- Indicate the objectives of your packaging (e.g., inform, educate, sell):

- Describe the information and graphics on the outer package (e.g., testimonials, list of benefits, image, awards, logos):

- Illustrate the package shape and size (e.g., rectangular, square, flat):

- Specify the materials that make up the outer package (e.g., cardboard, plastic, glass, metal):

- Describe the contents of the interior of your package (e.g., product, user manual, foam, cardboard):

Congratulations, you've completed the development step and are on your way to turning your idea into a successful product. Proceed to Step Six to launch your product!

Chapter 17
Step Six – Launch It

Most successful men have not achieved their distinction by having some new talent or opportunity presented to them. They have developed the opportunity that was at hand.

Bruce Marton

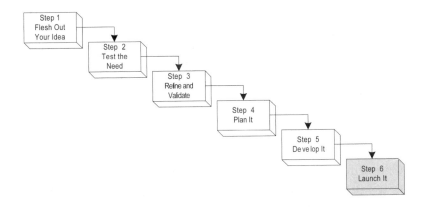

The sixth step of the **Market-Step** process is the product launch. Launch means introducing your product into the market. Some people use the term launch interchangeably with commercialize, first customer ship, general availability, or product kick-off. It's time to launch when the product has been produced and tested, and marketing and sales programs are ready.

Imagine launching a rocket. There's an enormous amount of activity involved – preparing the rocket, training astronauts, and developing lab experiments to test in space. Then comes the moment of truth – the launch. Blasting though the atmosphere, a sequence of actions are executed while progress is monitored. Course corrections are made as needed. When the spacecraft reaches orbit, the spacecraft is checked, and experiments are set up. Your product is about to launch into the hands of your customers. You'll make preparations and then obtain sales. And, you'll monitor progress and make changes as needed.

In Step Six, you'll:

1. Finalize product production, packaging, and documentation
2. Announce product availability
3. Implement marketing programs to induce awareness
4. Produce sales

If you're completing Step Six yourself, perform activities one through four in order. If you have two or more people, you can save time by working in tandem. A person or team can finalize the product, while others implement your marketing and sales programs.

Launch Strategy

When is your product ready to launch? A product that does not meet the perception of quality and fill a need will ultimately fail. Whoever tries your product and is disappointed is unlikely to give you another shot.

Sometimes a product has a deadline imposed by seasonal buying (e.g., Christmas), or an annual event (e.g., trade show). Waiting another year is often not a viable alternative. In this case, you may have to reduce the number of product features, packaging, documentation, or other issues that might delay product launch. But do not sacrifice quality. It's better to have fewer functions that work well than to have more that under-perform.

Where's a good place to introduce your product? Initially, focus on your local market, and then expand to regional and national markets. Within your local market, introduce your product where there's the greatest need.

Step Six – Product Launch Flowchart

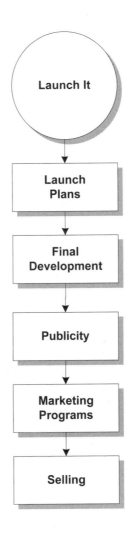

Competitor presence is a factor to consider. Competitors collectively stir up the market and this is good. But, if competitor presence is overwhelming, start at a different location. If your product is Internet-based, then physical geography is not an issue. But, place your messages where people have the greatest need.

Whom should you first target? Focus on Innovator and Early Adopters within your target market because they're less price sensitive and tend to be more forgiving of product deficiencies. They're eager to buy new products and you need to generate sales as quickly as possible.

Tailor communications to position your product as new and innovative. Exact messaging will depend on your target market. For example, attract them with messaging such as cool, innovative, newest technology, and stylish design. Even if your product does not involve new technology, there are people in every social group who are Early Adopters. And they're interested in new products that make them stand out from the crowd.

How do you actually find the Innovators and Early Adopters? It's not easy. As discussed earlier, marketing is part art and science. Your initial marketing might be scattered. But, as you generate sales, gather as much customer information as you can (e.g., job title, hobbies, geographic location, business type). Then, focus your marketing and sales to the types of buyers who have purchased your product. Keep narrowing your focus until you find your true target market.

If you're selling through retailers and distributors, who do you initially target? If you're selling through distribution channels, large retailers and distributors want to see a successful sales track record and evidence you can deliver on large orders. Start with small retail stores and distributors. Then work your way up to the next larger retailers and distributors.

In addition, your launch strategy must mirror the way customers buy. You'll want to communicate with customers at each stage of their buying process. Knowing the buying process works to your advantage when using the following marketing tactics to take a customer from awareness to purchase:

1. **Awareness** – Facilitate awareness with advertising, direct mail, press releases, product reviews, retail packaging, special events, and sales prospecting.
2. **Interest** – Generate excitement and interest with special deals, promotions, and strong benefit messages.
3. **Purchase** – Make your product available where your target market shops or at popular websites; offer a reasonable price; and a money-back guarantee.
4. **Satisfaction** – Create a product that performs as promised (meets or exceeds perceptions and expectations).
5. **Word of Mouth** – Provide a slogan, positioning statement, or concise statement of benefits that the customer can easily repeat to others.
6. **Re-order** – Get repeat orders by shipping your product with order forms, placing your telephone number and website address on your product, sending coupons, and mailing reminders.

Finalize Your Product

Monitor final development with the launch checklist you created earlier. If you're working with a number of people, the launch checklist serves as a sign-off from those responsible for development, marketing, quality assurance, and manufacturing. Review the following development items on a daily basis as you near launch.

- Parts ordering
- User documentation
- Product production
- Test results
- Packaging production

Your marketing and sales programs will need to be finalized so that they're ready to roll when the product is ready. Give yourself plenty of lead time to design, develop, edit, and submit each communications element. Organize these marketing and sales items before launch:

- Advertising (long lead times)
- Brochures
- Direct mail
- Press releases
- Sales letters
- Website

Countdown to Launch

Bring all these activities and elements together in the days leading up to the launch and the days that follow:

- Assemble product, packaging, and shipping materials.
- Submit a press release to an online press release service, as well as direct to your target audience magazines, newspapers, distributors, retailers, and upload to your website.
- Send a press kit or product launch kit to your distributors and retailers.
- Ship products to pre-arranged customers (e.g., samples and demos to end-users, distributors, and retailers).
- Make sales calls to prospects.
- Execute marketing programs such as postcard mailings, email blast to your personal list, or attend trade shows.

Announce the Launch with a Press Release

By the time the product is released from manufacturing, all marketing and sales activities should be planned and ready to execute. A press release is an announcement to the media to generate awareness.

Gain more press coverage by linking your product launch to a current or historical event. For example, if you've invented a new type of communications device, you could launch the same day Alexander Graham Bell invented the telephone. There are many historical events with anniversaries every day. Search the Internet using the keywords ["your product type" and "historical events"]. For example, in Google use the keywords ["light bulb" and "historical events"]. Then, look for events that are near your launch date.

The timing of your product launch may coincide with an event such as a trade show. In this case, your press release would announce that your new product will be unveiled at a particular trade show or conference. If you launch at a trade show, have signs at your booth highlighting your new product. In addition, ask the trade show managers about placing signs around the trade center, inserting flyers into show directories, or sponsoring a show event.

If your product has a long sales cycle, marketing and sales activities should begin months before the product is ready for commercial release. In this case, announce well in advance the launch date with a press release and notice on your website. For example, your message might be, "The General Availability of Product X will be October 1, 2004." If the launch date is uncertain, you can say for example, "Fall, 2004." And when the product is available, you might change your website to read, "Product X began shipping on October 1, 2004."

Press Release Submission

Today, a majority of press releases are submitted electronically. There are online press release distribution services that will take your press release and distribute it to many of the major news services and publications instantly.

Distribution services will forward your release to their member media organizations. Media organizations then review each press release and decide whether to publish it or not. Some distribution services are free and others charge up to $500. The paid services usually have a broader member base. Review the member list to make sure they include your target market before signing on with a distribution service. If the free services include your target market, start with them. Free and fee-based Internet press release distribution services include:

- Business Wire (www.businesswire.com)
- Emailwire (www.emailwire.com)
- !PR Services (www.exclamationpr.com)
- Press Release Network (www.pressreleasenetwork.com)
- PR Newswire (www.prnewswire.com)
- PR Web (www.prweb.com)
- Xpress Press (www.xpresspress.com)

In addition, send your press release to individual publications that serve your target market and cover your product type. Submitting directly increases your probable acceptance rate. Make a list of publications that might be interested and then search their website for "submit news" or "press release" or "submission process." They'll usually provide a form for your press release and contact information. To make it easy, cut and paste information from your word processor into the appropriate fields in their form.

Include photographs of your product, preferably taken by a professional photographer who'll provide the photographs as digital files. For press releases submitted by email, include product photos in high-resolution for print publications (300 dpi JPEG format), and low-resolution images for web display (72 dpi JPEG format). Some online forms will allow you to attach a photo to your press release.

Media publishers have lead times related to the frequency and size of the publication. For instance, quarterly publications generally have a three-month lead time. In this case, submit the press release three or four months before the launch date. On the other hand, daily newspapers or online publications may have a lead time of hours or days. In this case, indicate "For Immediate Release" at the top of the press release.

Press Release Format

FOR IMMEDIATE RELEASE:

CONTACT:
Contact person
Company name
Phone number
Fax number
Email address
Website address

Headline

City, State – Date – Opening Paragraph (inform that your new product is available)

Paragraph (key product advantages and benefits, where the product is available)

Paragraph (quotes from yourself or testimonials from known people)

Paragraph (summary of your company)

Closing sentence (should include your website address, contact name, phone, and email)

# # #
(indicates end of press release)

Press Release Format

A professional public relations person can write and submit a press release for you, but if you feel comfortable writing, make sure that you:

- Write concisely (one or two pages)
- Place key facts up front in the early paragraphs
- Avoid words that sound like advertising lingo

- Avoid jargon
- Include contact information

To help format your press release, look at others for your product type. Find these with an Internet search engine with keywords ["your product type" and "press release"].

If you print your press release, and there's more than one page, indicate "– more –" at the bottom of the first page, and "Page 2" at the top of the second page.

Supply Product Information

A press release provides basic information, but additional data is often needed. Depending on your product industry, you might need to create either a press kit or product launch kit.

Press Kit

A press kit, sometimes referred to as a media kit, brings together all your product and company information. Create a press kit that includes:

- **Fact sheet** – A summary of important company and product information.
- **Photographs** – You and your products, and possibly the output or results of your product.
- **Press releases** – Press releases that you have submitted
- **Product reviews** – Reviews of your product that have appeared in newspapers and magazines.
- **Press quotes** – Published product or company remarks made in newspapers and magazines (print and online).

Product Launch Kit

Your distributors, retailers, and customers might need detailed information about your product before they're persuaded to place an order. A product launch kit brings together important

---

Product Launch Kit

Use this template as a guide to creating your product launch kit.

Product Description
Describe your product in terms of benefits, features, and specifications:

Positioning
Indicate the product position in the market and advantages your product offers as compared to the competition:

Technology
Describe any technology that makes your product exciting:

Pricing
Either provide a price list or indicate customers should contact you or a sales representative directly:

Packaging
List part numbers, the contents of the package, and any available accessories and their part numbers. Also indicate the weight of the package individually and the weight of the master carton:

Ordering Instructions
Provide ordering instructions such as going to a website, placing a fax order, or by telephone:

Contact Information
List who to contact for more information. Include telephone numbers, email address, mailing address, and website:

---

information about your product. There's no standard format, but the product launch kit usually includes one document (printed or an electronic file) that provides key product, marketing, and sales information. In addition, the product launch kit may include product brochures, product reviews, product samples if appropriate, and competitive information.

Tip: Turn a press kit or product launch kit into electronic files that are downloadable from your website. Have a link on your home page to a page called "Press Room." On the "Press Room" page, allow downloads of your product launch kit, press releases, product reviews, fact sheets, and photos. This saves you the cost of printing, postage, and shipping materials. And, those interested can acquire the information instantly. At the same time, if your product has an expensive price tag you'll need to print a fancy color press kit to provide a perceived value of quality.

Advertising Builds Trust

Is advertising effective to generate awareness, create interest, and produce sales? We're influenced by advertising more than you think. The listing in the Yellow Pages for florists, the coupon in the newspaper for breakfast cereals, or the red car in a TV commercial – all these images stir our minds to think about a particular product when a buying situation occurs.

Advertising also builds comfort and familiarity and says you're not a stranger. You'll need to do this if your product or company is new or relatively unknown. Buyers will need to at least know *of* you before listening to your sales pitch or buying your product. In general, reasons to advertise include:

- Creating awareness, familiarity, credibility, and a positive reputation
- Directing people to a retail store, web store, or your website
- Influencing people who then influence your buyer
- Impressing the financial community when seeking investors
- Showing you're a serious player to distributors and retailers

Can advertising influence attitudes? At a business function, I was sitting at a table of computer programmers. They were looking through some magazines when one commented that lately he hadn't seen advertising from a particular company. Another programmer assumed that the company must not be doing so well. They all nodded their heads in agreement. Whether that company was doing well or not was not truly known. The fact that the company stopped advertising in a particular magazine sent a signal that the company was in trouble. The underlying message was "don't buy from them because they're likely going out of business."

Buying Advertising

Advertising is comprised of two elements — what you say and where you say it. There's no shortage of places to advertise. There are print media (e.g., magazines, newspapers), online media (e.g., click-through ads, click-through listings, and your website). Start by looking at where similar products are consistently advertised.

Often, if someone else is making money from a particular media, they'll stick with it. If their product isn't selling, they'll look elsewhere. For example, if a similar product is advertised in *Popular Mechanics*, go to a library to look at back issues. Many advertisers start with a three-to six-issue commitment. If you see the same ad in ten or more issues, then that medium is working for them.

A successful ad may be one that produces sales revenue that provides a return greater than the cost of ad placement. Some ads are successful when used in conjunction with other programs such as direct mail or telemarketing. If you see a consistently running ad for your product type, experiment by following their call to action such as visiting a website or calling a telephone number. See how they lead the audience through the sales process. It might be a method that you can use as a role model. Or, perhaps you'll learn what not to do.

Before buying advertising space, you'll want to know costs, demographics, and audience size. Usually, the more subscribers or number of hits on a website, the more expensive the advertising. Go to a publisher's website and look for "Advertising Info" or a similar link. Then look for "Media Kit" or "Advertising Kit" that includes rates and demographics. Review these demographics and compare them to your target market. If they match, you're on the right track; otherwise look somewhere else.

In general, it's better to place smaller ads for a long period rather than a large ad for a short period. Keep consistency in mind. It's a matter of timing. People are in different stages of their buying process. If they're gathering information at the same time your ad appears, they will contact you.

Closing dates are important. You'll probably need to submit your display ad one to three months before publication. Online advertising is faster.

In Chapter 15, we discussed setting a budget of about 25% of your expenditures for marketing communications. Of that, consider setting aside 20% to 50% for advertising. The actual amount depends on the competitive environment and nature of your product. Distribute your yearly budget into monthly segments to ensure consistent messaging.

Creating an Ad

Like marketing in general, ad creation is part art and part science. Successful ads depend on creativity and artistic skill to bring together certain psychological parameters that will appeal to your audience.

You'll generally need at least two people to create an ad—a copywriter and a designer. Use the following as a guide to creating print or online advertising.

- **Headline** – Attention-getting benefit or question that your target audience can identify with.
- **Image** – Include an image that depicts the results of using your product (e.g., a person smiling and no longer

worried about a situation), an image that only shows the product, or the product in use.

- **Description** – Indicate the type of product you're offering. Don't assume it's obvious from a picture.
- **Target Audience** – Mention the target audience by name so they know your product is for them (e.g., "The amazing screwdriver made specifically for Auto Mechanics outperforms …").
- **Solution** – Know your audience's problem and offer a solution.
- **Benefits** – Benefits sell. Be enthusiastic about the benefits derived from using your product (e.g., "Our new screwdriver cuts assembly time in half.").
- **Promotion** – People need a "call to action" inducement to contact you or place an order (e.g., send for a free booklet, buy now for a discount, or limited-time offer).
- **Next Step** – Explain how to take advantage of your offer (e.g., "Call our toll-free number for a free consultation.").
- **Contact Information** – Include telephone numbers, mailing address, email address, and website address.

Make sure your ads are honest and believable. Use facts, figures, and statistics to increase credibility. Remember the ad, "4 out of 5 dentists recommend ..."? The audience wants to know who else backs your product. Your ads should be coordinated with other elements of your marketing program so people can readily identify your product.

Effective Direct Mail

Direct mail involves one-to-one communication with current or future customers. The guidelines are essentially the same for direct mail and direct email, but with some subtle differences. When discussing direct mail in this section, I'm talking about both physical mail and email.

In the age of the Internet, don't think that having a website is enough. You'll still need to go out and get business. You cannot wait for customers to come to you. Direct mail can be used to generate awareness, direct people to your website, or induce people to call you. Many forms of direct mail work especially well when part of an integrated marketing campaign. Direct mail can be used to:

- Generate sales
- Announce product availability to generate leads
- Generate repeat sales
- Announce incentives to distributors and retailers

Direct mail can be very successful or fail miserably. You can expect an average response rate of 1%. In other words, for every one hundred direct mail pieces you send out, you'll get one person to respond. But 5% to 10% responses are possible with a very targeted mailing that includes a good offer. When direct mail fails, it's usually because of one or more of the following:

- The offer was not stimulating, meaning the offer was not conducive to motivate a response.
- The mail piece design was unappealing, not clear, or did not attract the recipient's attention.
- The list was comprised of the wrong audience.

The Direct Mail Offer

Think about direct mail you've received. Of the offers presented, what attracted your attention, and to which ones did you reply? Did you buy right away or did you need more information?

The sales process is either a one-step or multi-step process. For products that are known, easy to understand, and are reasonably priced, it's fine to ask for the sale in one-step. But for products that are new, perceived as complicated to use, or from an unknown company, asking for the order in your first communication is premature. Instead, you'll need to 1) generate a lead by direct mail, and then 2) cultivate a sale via a telephone call and/or other marketing programs.

To start the sales process, stimulate interest with an offer (e.g., free information or a free trial product). Prospective customers who receive your sample or information will start to warm up when they like what they see. Then, follow-up with questions and discuss terms of a purchase.

Sell the offer, *not* the product. Communicate the benefits of the offer and the steps customers will need to obtain the offer. Offers may include one or more of the following:

For multi-step sales:
- Free product trial
- Free product information
- Free initial consultation
- Free gift
- Free booklet with tips and tricks related to your product

For one-step sales:
- Discounts (e.g., 15% off, save $25)
- Get more product (e.g., buy one – get one free)
- Free shipping and handling
- Free bundled products or services

Asking for someone to call you or visit your website is *not* an offer. The offer must be a real benefit to recipients. Sometimes you have to experiment to discover which offer will stimulate the most response. Some people like free shipping, while others are attracted by a discount. But, all offers should have a time limit to induce a sense of urgency.

In addition to stating the offer, reinforce it with a visual representation. Show the product sample, booklet, or monetary savings. This will make your offer more tangible. For example, if your offer is buy two and get one free, then show three products with the word "Free" next to the image.

Once you've described your offer, you'll need explain the actions you want prospective customers to take. For example, "To take advantage of this special offer, fill out the enclosed card and place it in the postage-paid envelope." Mention the action step more than once so that it sinks in. Actions that you can ask include:

- Going to your website (e.g., to obtain your offer)
- Sending you an email
- Calling you
- Sending a fax
- Mailing a postcard or envelope
- Meeting you (e.g., trade show or seminar)

The Mail Piece

We're all barraged by direct mail. I'm sure you've received mail of all shapes, sizes, and colors. How will yours stand out? There are an assortment of direct mail possibilities at your disposal. The format and design of your direct mail should be based on your positioning, branding, and theme.

For example, if your product is positioned as high quality and expensive, your direct mail piece should be of the same high quality. Make sure that your direct mail's look and feel is consistent with other marketing programs. Work with your creative team to develop a direct mail piece that's professional and appealing to your target audience. Here are various direct mail formats you can use:

- Postcard
- Self-mailer
- Sales Letter
- Catalog
- Email

A classic direct mail piece is an envelope containing a sales letter, brochure, and reply card or reply envelope. The sales letter often generates the highest response rate but can be two to three times more expensive than a postcard or self-mailer. The extra expense is the postage, brochure, return card, or envelope, plus the time and effort to put them into envelopes.

The first thing you want people to do is open the envelope. Placing something inside the envelope will increase curiosity and attract attention. For example, National Pen Corporation places personalized pens inside an envelope. People feel something unusual and want to see what's inside. I suggest you place something inside that's intriguing or represents the positive results of using your product. Once the envelope is opened, your sales letter should entice the reader with an exciting offer.

Sales letters start by getting the reader's attention. This could be with a fantastic offer, description of product benefits, or a question. Posing a question often stimulates readers to formulate an answer. Next, you want to stimulate further interest by making an offer that is a real benefit to the reader. Keep the focus on benefits rather than features. In addition, anticipate questions and provide the answers. At the conclusion, clearly state how readers can receive your offer. Sign the letter and provide a postscript (P.S.). Research indicates that people who might otherwise skim your letter, will fully read a postscript. Therefore, use it to restate your offer or to emphasize your product's benefits.

For low costs and effectiveness, a postcard mailing is a great way to go. Postage is a little more than half the cost of a first-class letter, and there's no envelope stuffing and sorting. Limited space to promote your product is the one disadvantage, but that can be offset somewhat by using both sides effectively. On the front with the recipient address, place your headline. On the back, describe your product, its benefits, the offer, and most importantly, the next steps to take. Don't think that the postcard itself will sell your product. It's part of a two-or three-step process that will make prospective customers aware of your product. But make sure there's an offer and an action for the reader.

I like the combination of low cost and good response generated by a self-mailer. A self-mailer is essentially a brochure or newsletter that's folded in half or in thirds. It can also be a CD holder such as those sent by AOL. On the outside, the name and address of the recipient is printed or affixed with a label. On the inside is the message about your product and offer. I like self-mailers that include a postage-paid return postcard (response card). This format allows readers to respond easily. A person who returns a response card has some interest, but must receive a follow-up telephone call or email to qualify their needs and wants. A self-mailer is not as personal as a letter, but can communicate well in a multi-step sale process.

For email, follow the same guidelines as physical direct mail except for the following: Your email should state the headline in the subject line. Place a date in the body of the message. Keep content short and to the point. Place your website address and business address at the beginning *and* end of the email. And, allow the recipient to unsubscribe or remove from the list at any time.

On the Internet, people are looking for information and tend to skip over advertisements. I suggest you send a direct email containing mostly information such as tips and how-to's. And at the end of the email, provide a special offer and action steps to obtain your offer. Your objective is keeping your product in the mind of the potential customer. When they're ready to buy, they'll consider you as a source.

Some additional tips to increase direct mail response:

- Write a sales letter as if you're writing to one person rather than to a group. Personalize a letter with the person's name rather than using "Dear Friend." Use sentences that are personal such as "You'll be interested…" rather than "Everyone will be interested…".
- Write paragraphs that are indented and use a left justification only. Limit your use of bold and underlined words.
- Use certain words that trigger positive responses (e.g., benefit, free, guarantee, how to, limited, new, only, proven, save, special, unique).
- People are savvier today and can see through inflated claims. Use facts and specific numbers in your descriptions.

- For a personalized mailing, use a regular postage stamp rather than bulk mail mark. This increases costs but might increase revenue. This is impractical of course if you're mailing tens of thousands of letters.
- When selling expensive items, use Business Reply Mail in which potential customers do not have to pay postage for cards or envelopes returned. Talk to your local post office or view their website (www.usps.gov) about the Business Reply process.
- During a mail crisis such as the anthrax mailings, people were afraid to open letters when they didn't know the sender. Under these conditions, mail postcards only.
- If exhibiting at a trade show, send a pre-show personalized letter with an invitation to come to your booth for a free gift and product information at least ten days before the event.
- If you're selling a product to business and there are multiple people in an organization that could benefit from your product, target the highest-ranking person in their hierarchy who understands the problem your product solves.

The Mailing List

Having the right mailing list is one of the keys to direct mail success. The ideal list includes prospects that represent your target audience, are influenced by direct mail, and are ready to buy. Knowing when they're ready to buy is unknown unless market research indicates that your target market buys your type of product at a certain time (e.g., buying a bicycle for a child at Christmas or flowers for Mother's Day).

You can create a mailing list yourself, trade with another company, or rent one. Lists are created by list brokers who rent them at a cost on average of $25 to $100 per 1,000 names. This price is for one-time use. To prevent re-use, lists contain a few dummy names to monitor the mailing. For multiple mailings you'd pay a negotiated rate. Note, however, that you own the name of anyone who responds to your direct mail and may freely use it in future mailings. There are many list brokers who want to rent you their lists. To get an idea of what they provide, visit Dun & Bradstreet's Zapdata (www.zapdata.com), Info USA (www.infousa.com), or Direct Media (www.directmedia.com). In addition, if your product fits well with a particular magazine or trade journal, contact them to see if they'll rent subscriber names.

Lists are provided on mailing labels that you stick to your mail piece or as electronic files. Some files are provided on a CD, tape, or can be downloaded. I suggest you obtain electronic files so that you can personalize your letters. To personalize your letters use a program such as Microsoft Word that has mail merge capability. Mail merge is a method that combines database fields such as name, address, city, state, and zip code with a document.

Rented lists are either "compiled" or "response." Compiled lists come from public records on people and businesses, the phone book, court records, etc. A compiled list is good when targeting a household or business of a known size, income level, or location. For example, if your target market is owners of boats over fifty feet long, you can get this list from a direct mail database company that has compiled lists from boat sellers.

Response lists are based on people who have made previous purchases from catalogs, magazines, retail stores, and others. For example, response lists are good if your target audience matches the profile of the readers of a particular magazine who have purchased a subscription. There's a good chance that if your product matches the magazine's content, readers will be a good target. In general, response lists are often twice as expensive as a compiled list but worth the extra cost.

Ultimately, you'll want to build your own list to use over and over again. People who respond to any of your marketing programs become part of a valuable list. One method of adding people is from those who choose to sign-up at your website. Your offer might be a free newsletter, free tips, free giveaway, or a membership to access your website. Make it clear that you'll keep the information private. The more information you ask for, the greater your risk of scaring people away. I prefer to personalize email with a first name. Therefore, the only information I request is a first name and email address. If you need additional information I suggest making that optional.

If you have a customer list of your own, you could trade your list with another company. There's probably another company catering to the same target market with a non-competing product. For example, you're selling toys for pets and another company is selling pet food. If you do not yet have a list and they do, offer to share the cost of a mailing to sell both of your products. In addition, if you're selling through a distributor or retailer, ask to send out direct mail jointly to their customer list.

How many mailings should you send? Part of the answer depends on your budget, the other part on how many sales will deem your direct mail program a success. For your budget of printed mailings, figure an average cost of one dollar per name.

Consider how many responses you can handle. If 1% of the list calls or emails you during the course of a week, do you have the ability to respond to the phone calls or emails? You can either hire additional people, or consider staggering the mailing over a number of weeks.

Direct mail fulfillment companies will print, assemble, and mail for you. They're worth using, especially for large mailings. For companies that help with direct mail in your area, look in the Yellow Pages under Mailing Lists or Advertising – Direct Mail.

Direct Mail Timing

Certain months work better than others for direct mail. In general, the beginning of the year, January through March, are good months for mailings. On the other hand, the summer months, June through August, are usually poor response months. These are general assumptions, but it's likely that your target market has a buying season. For example, if you were selling umbrellas, mailings would be timed for the beginning of the rainy season.

You must find out by asking some members of the target market when they usually buy your type of product. Your target market might need your product for an event such as a holiday season, trade show, or when new budgets are made.

Frequency is another important timing aspect to consider. Maybe your first mailing reached someone on a bad day. Or, at that time there was no need. After the first mailing, send a second mail piece three weeks later and a third in three months. Each follow-up mailing should have the same offer but a slight format or message change.

If you send out email newsletters, the current research states that every two to three weeks is an effective frequency. My personal research seems to suggest that potential customers need to receive your message up to seven times by email before a response. But you never know when they're ready to buy. I suggest creating a newsletter with a few tips and tricks related to your product. But keep the offer the same over a three-month period. Change the offer every three months.

Direct Mail Math

Does direct mail make sense financially? You'll need to do the math. On the expense side there's design, production, postage, and cost of the mailing list. On the revenue side, a purchase response of 1% to 2% is thought to be typical. But for very targeted lists, 10% response is possible. I suggest you start your calculations with conservative numbers.

For example, you send a mailing to 10,000 people. Two percent respond by calling and emailing for more information (10,000 x 2% = 200 people). Of those 200 people, 100 make a purchase. Your product sells for $150. Therefore, 100 sales times a selling price of $150 produces revenue of $15,000. If your product costs are $25 each, then your net profit is $2,500 as summarized on the following page.

Gross Profit
- Mail to 10,000 people
- 2% respond by requesting more information: 10,000 x 2% = 200 people
- Of the 200 people, half of them buy = 100 unit sales
- Revenue = selling price of $150 x 100 unit sales = $15,000
- Product unit costs = $25 x 100 unit sales = $2,500
- Gross profit = Sales revenue – Product unit costs
- Therefore, Gross profit = $15,000 – $2,500 = $12,500

Expenses
- Direct mail costs for the mail piece, postage, and list comes to $1 each for a total of $10,000

Net Profit
- Net Profit = Gross profit – Expenses = $12,500 – $10,000
- Therefore, Net Profit = $2,500

In this example, you would earn $2,500. But, over time, as more people become familiar with your product, you'll get more response. And then when you satisfy customers, free word-of-mouth advertising and referrals are possible. For more information and tips on direct mail, visit the Direct Marketing Association website (www.the-dma.org).

Personal Selling

Selling is the process of facilitating a transaction – your product in exchange for money. Uncovering market needs from a sales viewpoint is commonly known as prospecting. Prospecting may include making outbound calls, meeting people face-to-face, and answering inbound calls.

Part of the selling process involves creating the proper mindset. We can become anxious when promoting our product because it may feel like there's a lot on the line. When you converse with someone in person, email, or on the telephone, your objective is to reduce pressure. People will shift into defensive mode if they think you're selling something. They do not want to be sold, they want to buy. You must adopt the role of problem solver. Instead of approaching someone with the intent to sell, which also puts pressure on you, just go into the situation to figure out if there's a need. You have no agenda other than to ask questions. Tell the person you're there to provide education about your product. If they have a need for your product, great, if not, that's okay too.

To get started, you'll want to build a contact list. Start with your beta testers, focus group attendees, and survey recipients. Then add those who respond to your press release, advertising, direct mail, trade shows, free newsletter on your website, and other marketing programs.

To manage this information (e.g., names, addresses, telephone numbers, and email addresses) you'll need to set up a contact database. There are many contact databases available and some of the better known are *Act!* and *SalesLogix* from Best Software, *Goldmine* from Front Range Solutions, and *Maximizer* by Multiactive. If you have Microsoft Office, Outlook and Excel provide a reasonable method of tracking customers.

Launch Conclusion

Launching a new product is like giving birth to a child. When a child is born, you don't say, "Okay, it's born, my job is finished." Now is the time to nourish it, promote it, and earn the rewards from your hard work. Your customer wins with a great product. You win by knowing you're helping others and by making money for yourself. Congratulations, you have finally realized your vision and have launched your product!

Chapter 18
Post-Launch Progress Check

If everything seems under control, you're just not going fast enough.

Mario Andretti

After launching your product, you'll need to monitor marketing and sales effectiveness. This involves analyzing marketing and sales activities to determine if you'll need to change product functionality, positioning, pricing, selling, or marketing.

Marketing and Sales Analysis

Marketing and sales analysis will help you determine if the unit volume or revenue is meeting your objectives. Think of the buying process. If you're not getting leads, there's a problem creating awareness. If you're getting leads, but only a small number are converting to sales, your sales methods might need improvement. If your product is a consumable that people would need to re-order and they're not, there could be a problem with the product or the re-ordering process.

To identify trends, keep track of the following marketing and sales activities by placing them into a log using a program such as Microsoft Excel:

- Date marketing program publicly appears
- Marketing program (e.g., email to your newsletter subscribers, direct mail to *Popular Mechanics* subscribers, or Google keywords)
- Number of leads generated (e.g., email requests for more information, website hits, calls in response to an

advertisement, direct mail response cards received, or contacts made at a trade show)
- Number of units sold
- Revenue generated
- Cost of marketing program

Marketing and Sales Log					
Date	Marketing Program	Leads	Units Sold	Revenue	Cost

Sales Losses

Another way to fine-tune your product and business practices is to ask questions of those who decided not to buy. When it seems apparent that a prospective customer will not buy your product, call and ask why. Let them know that you realize you can't help them with your product, and that's okay. You just want to know the honest reason why they did not buy. Whatever they tell you, do not defend yourself, just listen. Use this feedback to enhance your product, your marketing, and sales methods. Questions to ask include:

- Did you buy another product?
- What was your biggest complaint about our product?
- Was our company easy to work with?
- What improvements would you suggest?

To conclude, thank them for their time and give them your name and telephone number in case they have not purchased another product or become dissatisfied with the competitor's product.

Customer Satisfaction

You might assume that people love your product for one reason, but they really like something else instead. For example, I figured customers purchased my wireless modem because of the remote capabilities, pricing, and ease of use. Yes, those were strong factors, but 24-hour support was the deciding purchase factor because it gave customers peace of mind. As a result, I emphasized 24-hour support in future marketing messages.

Customer feedback in the form of surveys (mail or email) or telephone calls reveal how they're using your product and provide suggestions for improvements. I suggest surveying all customers and then call a few.

Call customers and ask why they purchased your product. They may be surprised you're calling, but some will be eager to talk. First, thank them for purchasing your product. Inform them that you're seeking feedback to improve the product. Let them know you only have a few questions, but ask if this is a good time. Questions to ask include:

- What was your reason for buying the product?
- Why did you choose the product over others?
- What do you primarily use the product for (if it's not obvious)?
- What type of business are you in (if selling to businesses)?
- What, if any, improvements would you suggest?
- Has the company been easy to work with?

To conclude, thank them for their time and provide your name and phone number in case they have questions or come up with suggestions later.

Competition Review

How has the competition reacted to your product? Different competitors will react differently. They might:

- Change their product price
- Talk about your product in a disparaging way
- Change their marketing and sales strategies and tactics
- Add or change product features
- Do nothing

Monitor competitors on a regular basis. Pick a day once a month to visit competitor websites to read their press releases, product information, and financial information. If they offer a newsletter or automatic email service, sign up for it.

Product Review

The information you collect from the customer feedback, sales, marketing, and competitive analysis will help you figure out what to improve for your next product release. If there are product defects that are causing poor reviews, lost sales, or product returns, then resolve the issue and re-launch the product as a new version.

Make product improvements to stay competitive and only if they'll have an impact on future sales. When customers and prospects make suggestions, ask if they'd still buy the product without this feature. If the answer is yes, then it may be unnecessary to include that feature in the next product version.

To create an updated product version, go through the **Market-Step** process again. It will be easier the next time around.

APPENDICES

I never perfected an invention that I did not think about in terms of the service it might give others. I find out what the world needs. Then I go ahead and try to invent it.

Thomas A. Edison

A: Investigate Your Competition
B: Select Your Target Market
C: The Market-Step Product Plan
D: Product Math
E: Funding Your Idea
F: Business Startup
G: Non-Disclosure Agreement

Appendix A
Investigate Your Competition

A competitor is any company or individual that supplies a similar product to your target market. You'll want to perform competitive research to know how to outsell them. In addition, if you seek funding or licensing, you'll need to explain your product's advantages over the competition and how you'll sustain those advantages.

To understand your competition, you'll need to know details about competitors and their products. This information will provide important insight about how to minimize competitive threats. In the next five sections, I'll walk you through the process of researching and analyzing competition.

List Competitors

Start by making a list of your potential competitors. Research of competitors includes trade magazines that have annual product lists, and Internet product or company directories. Yahoo (www.yahoo.com) is a great place to see companies listed by category. In addition, use the free patent search engine to find competitors with similar products (www.uspto.gov). Another free online service is Webster's Online (www.webdir.net).

You can also effectively search for competitors using the North American Industry Classification System (NAICS). NAICS provides categories and statistics of business activities in North America. This system is slowly replacing the Standard Industrial Code (SIC). Use NAICS to find lists of companies that sell products similar to yours. The United States Census Bureau maintains NAICS and is described in more detail on their website (www.census.gov/epcd/www/naics.html). In addition, the NAICS Association has a free search engine (www.naics.com).

To use the NAICS, first find the classification for your product type. For example, if your product is a screwdriver, go to their website (www.naics.com), click on NAICS Search, enter "screwdriver" and note the returned code, 333991. Using this code, go to Webster's Online and search by NAICS code. When you enter 333991, screwdriver manufacturers will be listed.

You might have many competitors. But, you are mainly concerned about companies that will give you the most competition. Key competitors are those that offer quality products with a known brand name, provide good value, have a large share of customers, or have growing revenue. Narrow your list to your key competitors:

Competitive Products and Prices		
Company	Product	Price

Collect Detailed Data

Using your list of key competitors, collect company and product details. Read product reviews in magazines or online, visit your competitors' websites, read their press releases, talk to marketing consultants, talk to sales people where the product is sold, and last but not least, use their product.

For computer products and accessories, check the CNET website (www.cnet.com) for its large database of reviews. You might also pay attention to Internet discussions on *Yahoo Groups* or *Google Groups* that mention what people like and do not like about particular products. Also, if a competitor is a public company, get their annual report and 10k reports. Study these reports for product information, discussions of competition, and financial statements. As you gather information, think of the following:

- Why do customers buy the competitor's product (e.g., brand name, quality, price, service, innovation, style)?
- What are the unique features of my product versus the competition?
- What are the deficiencies of my product versus the competition?

Reasons People Buy from the Competition	
Product	Reasons People Buy This Product

Organize Data

After you've gathered competitive information, you'll need to organize and summarize it. This information will be used when we determine how to combat your competition. For the company(s) that will give you the most competition (known brand, most customers, highest revenue, highest quality products) use the following format.

Summary of Each Key Competitor
Company name:
Product name(s):
Website address:
Stock symbol (if public):
Year founded:
Target market:
Perception in the market:
Product positioning:
Product pricing:
Marketing programs in use:
Distribution method:
Product strengths:
Product weaknesses:

Evaluate the Competitive Environment

The **Market-Step** Competitive Evaluation is a look at competition as a whole. For each question on the next page, check the box that best describes your competitive situation. Answering these questions will reveal your competitive environment.

For example, in "Number of Competitors" if there is only one competitor, put a checkmark in the box under "Few." Also, for insight into answering questions about market growth and market size, see Chapter 6 "The Role of Product Marketing."

Look at your checkmarks. If most are positioned on the right side, then your product is in a desirable competitive environment. If most checkmarks are positioned on the left side, then your product is in an undesirable environment and you'll need ways to combat your competition.

Competitive Evaluation				
[Undesirable]				[Desirable]
	Number of Competitors			
Many	(e.g., 30 is many, 3 is a few)			Few
❑	❑	❑	❑	❑
	Dominant Competitors			
Many	(large market share and known brand names)			None
❑	❑	❑	❑	❑
	Competitive Fighting			
Intense	(frequent marketing promotions, price wars)			Mild
❑	❑	❑	❑	❑
	Market Growth			
Shrinking	(average is 5%, high growth is 25% per year)			Growing
❑	❑	❑	❑	❑
	Market Size			
Small	(100 customers can be small, 100,000 is big)			Big
❑	❑	❑	❑	❑

Combat Competitors

When competition is intense, your product needs competitive advantages to entice prospective customers. There are a number of areas to combat competitors. Your competitive advantage might include one or more of the following:

- Lower price (along with your lower costs)
- Higher price based on quality, exclusivity, or luxury

- Greater product benefits
- Demonstrated higher quality
- Innovative features or style
- Greater overall value using a mix of features, quality, and price
- Better availability or convenience
- Excellent customer service
- Better marketing communications (e.g., advertising, promotions)
- Greater sales activity (e.g., more people, more territories)

What advantages does your product idea offer compared to the competition (e.g., faster, less expensive, longer lasting, higher quality, makes more money, saves more time, more fun, greater safety)? Inform your prospective customers about these advantages in your website, sales letter, brochure, and other communications.

Competitive Advantages	
Product	Your Advantage

You can also combat competitors by uncovering the weaknesses in their strengths. Companies often rely heavily on their strengths to win sales. So, if you can find fault with their strengths you have an advantage. For example, if your competitor is claiming their product has more features, you could communicate that all those extra features are a disadvantage because they're harder to learn, increase costs, and slow users down. Or, if a competitor claims their product is more technically advanced, you could point out that some advanced products are more complicated, harder to use, and are more prone to failure. List what your competition boasts as their best product assets, and think how that could be communicated to your prospective customers as a weakness.

Strengths Into Weaknesses	
Comp. Product	Their Strengths into Weaknesses

In summary, use your competitive investigation to create advantages in product design as well as marketing and sales strategies. Think like a competitor. What they would do if your product hit the market? Would they lower prices, add new features, or increase marketing? You'll want to create countermeasures ahead of time so that you can initiate actions rapidly to offset competitor moves.

Appendix B
Select Your Target Market

A target market is a market segment that you can best serve and earn the highest possible profit. A target market can be a group of people or businesses sharing common characteristics such as hobbies, occupations, or industry. For example, a target market could be coin collectors, female golfers, or computer manufacturers. These broad segments can be further narrowed down to coin collectors who live in San Francisco, female golfers over age 55 who live in Texas, or computer manufacturers with 1,000 or more employees.

Initially, you might have many market segments of people or businesses potentially interested in your idea. That's good, but you'll want to narrow that down to one market segment. Your target market is the one segment you intend to market and sell to. Choose a target market according to its potential for success. If you measure success in terms of profit, then your target market is the one that will deliver the greatest profits.

You need to select a target market because you do not have the time and money to sell to everyone. For example, if your product is golf clubs, you could not afford to advertise in every magazine and newspaper in print and online. While you could advertise golf clubs in a hockey magazine because some hockey players play golf, you can be sure advertising in a golf magazine will best reach your target audience.

Selecting a target market allows you to design a product with benefits and features that will appeal to your specific audience. Don't try to be everything to everybody.

The following diagram illustrates the process you'll use to select a target market. From the entire market, you'll brainstorm a few segments that might be the best source of sales. Next, you'll analyze each segment and identify the most attractive segment as the target market.

Markets and Segments

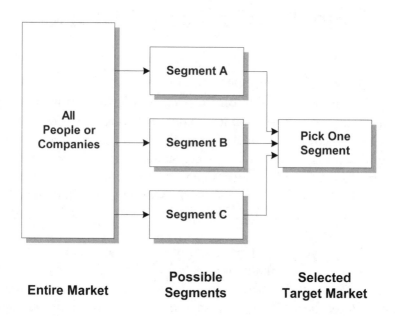

| Entire Market | Possible Segments | Selected Target Market |

Target Market Factors

When you have different market segments to consider, a few factors need examining because each target market factor can influence your choice. Let's look at the following factors, and then use them to select your target market.

- **Segment Size** – A measurement of the total number of people or companies in a market segment.
- **Buyer Interest** – The result of your interviews and surveys of a particular market segment. It's the percentage of those who have responded favorably.
- **Segment Potential** – The total number of potential interested buyers in each market segment. Segment Potential equals the Segment Size multiplied by the

percentage of Buyer Interest. We use the word "potential" because we don't know the exact number.

- **Buyer Price Sensitivity** – The selling price a market segment is willing to pay. Some segments of buyers will only buy something if it's on sale or there's a deep discount. For others, if you show that your product satisfies a need or saves money, they'll pay any reasonable price.
- **M/S Expense** – The marketing and sales expenses needed to reach a market segment. The less the expense the more favorable.
- **Market Growth** – An indicator of how fast the market is growing in terms of people or companies. For example, Las Vegas is a fast-growing city. So if your idea meets a need for people or companies in Las Vegas, then market growth is in your favor.
- **Buyer Readiness** – The time it takes for a customer to make a purchase. For example, if you're selling to a market segment consisting mainly of bureaucracies, purchase decisions could take a long time. Market segments that make quick purchase decisions are more desirable.
- **Competitiveness** – The number of competitors and the fierceness of the competition. Will your segment require you to compete with Sony, Panasonic, and Sanyo? Or, can you tailor your idea to a segment where there are no major players?
- **Familiarity** – The degree to which you understand the workings of a market segment. Market segments where you're familiar with the technology, trends, distribution, and customer behavior are more desirable.

Methods to Select a Target Market

There are two methods that I've developed to select a target market. The first is the **Market-Step** Profit Potential Method, which is a calculation of profit in each market segment. The market segment with the highest profit potential becomes your target market. We'll go through an example and then have you perform this calculation later.

Profit Potential Method

Use the following steps to determine the profit potential of a market segment:

1. **Segmentation** – Make a list possible market segments.
2. **Determine Segment Size** – The total number of people or companies in each market segment.
3. **Determine Buyer Interest** – The percent interest from concept surveys and interviews in each market segment.
4. **Calculate Segment Potential** – Multiply Segment Size by percentage of Buyer Interest.
5. **Determine a Selling Price** – Use survey information and comparative competitor pricing as a starting point to determine a selling price.
6. **Calculate Potential Revenue** – Multiply Segment Potential by Selling Price.
7. **Calculate Segment Profit** – Revenue Potential minus Unit Costs and M/S Expenses.

If one market segment has the highest profit potential, then this is your target market. If more than one market segment has comparable profit potential, then use the following Positive Factors Method to determine a target market.

Positive Factors Method

The second way to determine a target market is the **Market-Step** Positive Factors Method, which is the total number of favorable target market factors. This method is used to support your profit potential calculations.

Use the target market factors and rank each segment based on how it favors you. For each factor use a "+" if that factor favors you, a "o" if that factor is neutral, or "–" if the factor does not favor you. Therefore, a segment with the most plusses and least minuses is the most attractive market segment and is your target market. The Positive Factors Method uses the following target market factors:

- **Segment Size** – The larger the better.
- **Buyer Interest** – The higher percentage the better.
- **Buyer Price Sensitivity** – The higher the selling price the better.
- **M/S Expense** – The lower the marketing and sales expense the better.
- **Market Growth** – The greater the market growth the better.
- **Buyer Readiness** – The faster a customer takes to make a purchase the better.
- **Competitiveness** – The less intense and least amount of name brand competitors the better.
- **Your Familiarity** – The more familiar with a market segment the better.

Example of Market Segments for Screwdrivers

Let's use a new type of screwdriver for our example. You believe that the market segments are Carpenters, Auto Mechanics, and Homeowners over the age of 65. The next step is to determine the size for each of these market segments. Using the Internet, the library, or other research tools, look for the total number of people in each group. Use keywords such as "market size" or "market growth" in a search engine. For Carpenters, a search might be ["market size" and "carpenters"].

In this example, use the following market research assumptions to select a target market.

- **Segment Size** – Assume your research reveals that there are five hundred thousand Auto Mechanics, one million Carpenters, and ten million Homeowners over the age of

65 in this country. These numbers represent the segment size.

- **Buyer Interest (Percent)** – From conversations, interviews, and surveys, you conclude that 80% of Auto Mechanics would like the new screwdriver, as well as 30% of Carpenters, and 10% of Homeowners over the age of 65.
- **Number of Interested Buyers** – To determine the number of potential interested buyers, multiply the segment size times the percentage of interested buyers. This is an estimate of how many people are interested in your idea in each market segment.

		Segment Size	Buyer Interest	Interested Buyers
Auto Mechanics	=	500,000	80%	400,000
Carpenters	=	1,000,000	30%	300,000
Homeowners 65+	=	10,000,000	10%	1,000,000

Given these numbers, you might automatically assume that the homeowners market is your target market. But, other factors such as marketing and sales expenses, and price sensitivity, will influence your decision.

Let's calculate the profit potential for the Auto Mechanic segment.

- Assuming the appropriate Selling Price for this segment is $25, then Revenue is the number of Interested Buyers times the Selling Price which is 400,000 x $25 = $10,000,000.
- You estimate that your Unit Costs are $4 each, so then the Total Unit Costs is the number of Interested Buyers times the Unit Cost which is 400,000 x $4 = $1,600,000.
- You estimate that your M/S Expense to reach this market segment is $1,400,000.
- Therefore, Segment Profit is Revenue minus Total Unit Costs minus M/S Expenses which is $10,000,000 – ($1,600,000 and $1,400,000) = $7,000,000.

Performing the same calculations for each segment reveals that the Auto Mechanics would likely be the most profitable.

Target Market Selection by Profit Potential Method			
	1	2	3
Segment Choices	Auto Mechanics	Carpenters	Homeowners 65+
Segment Size:	500,000	1,000,000	10,000,000
x % Interest:	80%	30%	10%
= Potential:	400,000	300,000	1,000,000
x Selling Price:	$25	$20	$10
= Revenue:	$10,000,000	$6,000,000	$10,000,000
- Unit Costs:	$1,600,000	$1,200,000	$4,000,000
- M/S Expenses:	$1,400,000	$1,800,000	$5,000,000
= Profit:	$7,000,000	$3,000,000	$1,000,000
Your Selection	✓		

Let's look at the second method to determine a target market. Positive Factors Method uses target market factors to select a target market. Each factor is equally weighted in importance.

Recall that Auto Mechanics were very interested in the new screwdrivers. Therefore, you entered a "+" next to Buyer Interest. In terms of marketing and sales expenses, you telephoned the most popular trade journals in each of the three market segments. Advertising in the auto mechanic trade magazines is the least expensive out of the three segments. As a result, you entered a "+" next to M/S Expenses. The same research is performed for each factor.

Looking at the following table, you see that the Auto Mechanic segment has the most positive factors and least amount of negative factors. Therefore it is the target market.

To summarize this example, you started with the thought that there are three market segments: Carpenters, Auto Mechanics, and Homeowners over the age of 65. Then, you evaluated each segment by determining a profit potential. Then, you evaluated each by rating the positive target market factors. The most profitable and most favorable led you to conclude that Auto Mechanics are the best target market.

Target Market Selection by Positive Market Factors			
Segment Choices	1 Auto Mechanics	2 Carpenters	3 Homeowners 65+
Segment Size:	o	o	+
Buyer Interest:	+	o	–
Price Sensitivity:	+	+	–
M/S Expenses:	+	o	+
Market Growth:	o	+	+
Buyer Readiness:	+	o	–
Competitiveness:	o	+	o
Your Familiarity:	+	o	o
Total +	5	3	3
Total –	0	0	3
Score	5	3	0
Your Selection	✓		

Your Target Market

Now it's your turn to select a target market. Use the information from your market research, surveys, and interviews to determine a target market. Use the Profit Potential Method and Positive Factors Method as a guide.

Target Market Selection by Profit Potential Method

Segment Choices	1	2	3
Segment Size:			
x % Interest:			
= Potential:			
x Selling Price:			
= Revenue:			
– Unit Costs:			
– M/S Expenses:			
= Profit:			

Your Selection

Target Market Selection by Positive Market Factors

Segment Choices	1	2	3
Segment Size:			
Buyer Interest:			
Price Sensitivity:			
M/S Expenses:			
Market Growth:			
Buyer Readiness:			
Competitiveness:			
Your Familiarity:			
Total +			
Total –			
Score			

Your Selection

Other Targeting Methods

Selecting a target market is not an exact science. Selection is part planning, part experience, and part experimentation. In addition to the methods already described, here are a few others to try:

- **Method A** – Target several markets at once and narrow the choice down to the one that produces the best results. For example, select the three most likely market segments. Then, divide your marketing budget and apply one-third to each segment. Use the marketing communication tools discussed in Chapter 15 to create awareness, lead generation, and sales in each segment. Set a time limit such as six months. The type of customers who have generated the majority of revenue becomes your target market.

- **Method B** – Offer your product only on your website. Register your website with various search engines and see what type of people arrive. Have a form that allows people to request product information. One of the questions on the form asks demographic information such as job title, industry, age range, or other information that you'll need to narrow your market selection. Review the characteristics of those who have generated the majority of revenue to select a target market.

- **Method C** – Select the same target market as the leading competitors. Most likely your competitors have tried other markets and have found that the current market they serve is the best. But you'll need to offer some advantages to offset the awareness and reputation of the competition. As you acquire customers, find out from them how to improve the product and possibly discover other markets where you can serve.

Appendix C
The Market-Step Product Plan

A business plan is used to raise money or guide business operations. While a business plan provides a good overview for each product, a practical plan is needed to guide the details of a product launch. The **Market-Step** Product Plan provides a clear understanding of how your product meets the needs of customers, how you'll market it, and how you'll produce sales. The flow of the **Market-Step** Product Plan includes:

- **Uncovering the Facts** – Market need, market environment, and customer characteristics
- **Creating a Vision** – Goals, objectives, and strategies
- **Actions** – Marketing and sales tactics by sales cycle
- **Checking** – Monitoring and evaluating progress

There are nine sections to the **Market-Step** Product Plan. Read the descriptions and examples in each section, and then write your plan. A **Market-Step** Product Plan template is available on my website (www.MattYubas.com).

Market-Step Product Plan Contents

1. Purpose
2. Market Need
   2.1. Need
   2.2. Gap
   2.3. Solution
3. Market Environment
   3.1. Market Segments
   3.2. Market Segment Size

Market-Step Product Plan Sections

1. Purpose

Purpose is a statement that communicates the product plan's intent to investors, advisors, management, partners, or co-workers.

- Describe the purpose of your product plan.
- For example: "This document is a product marketing plan to launch our new TurboX toy."

2. Market Need

Market need describes the need for your type of product, the gap that currently exists in the market, and how your product fills the gap to solve the problems or satisfy a need or want.

2.1. Need

Need is the key problem, need, or want currently unmet. Either people are aware of their needs or sometimes must be shown how your product uncovers something missing in their lives.

- Describe the need for your type of product.
- For example: "In the toy market, children easily get bored with their toys. They want a product that can morph into a new look and function with interchangeable parts. They want a toy that does not fall apart."

2.2. Gap

Gap is a weak solution offered by competition or a lack of any solution.

- Compare what customers need and want, to what's currently available.
- For example: "Toys for male children break easily and are considered boring after just one hour. Parents

become frustrated about purchasing a toy the child no longer uses."

2.3.   Solution

A solution provides a person or organization with something that is better, is faster, reduces pain, raises esteem, provides increased safety, generates more revenue, cuts costs, or provides higher value to their customers.

- Describe how your product solves the customer's problems, fills the gap, and is better than other available products. Also, name support services or other products that must be included to provide a complete solution.
- For example: "The TurboX uses the latest high-strength plastics for long-term durability. Extra durability makes small interchangeable parts possible. These interchangeable parts allow for new features and functions in an almost unlimited set of configurations."

3.   Market Environment

The market environment is the arena where your product type competes for customer attention. It includes your customer market segments, market trends, market drivers, competitors, and industry influencers.

3.1.   Market Segments

A market segment is a group of customers with common characteristics, needs, and wants. Market segments include industry type, location, buyer preferences, and age. A target market is a market segment that you can best serve and earn the highest possible profit.

- Name possible market segments your product fits into. Evaluate a few market segments that may serve as a target market. Then evaluate each segment based on market size, revenue potential, opportunities, and threats.

- For example: "The potential market segments for the TurboX are single mothers, single fathers, or married couples. In all segments, there's at least one male child between the ages of five and ten."

3.2.   Market Segment Size

Market segment size is the total number of people or organizations within a market segment.

- Determine the size of each of your market segments.
- For example: "There are 15 million single mothers, 10 million single fathers, and 50 million married families."

3.3.   Market Segment Revenue Potential

Revenue potential is the total possible revenue from a market segment. Revenue potential is derived by the total number of potential buyers multiplied by the rate of purchase and multiplied by the product selling price.

- Calculate the maximum revenue potential (forecast) on a yearly basis, in each market segment, over the next three years. If you do not know a selling price, use an average amount of competitors or similar products.
- For example: "Revenue Potential = 10 million (potential buyers) x 2 (purchases per year) x $1 (selling price) = $20 million."

3.4.   Opportunities

Opportunities are new trends from government regulations, economic changes, new technology, and social changes.

- Name the opportunities in the marketplace for your type of product.

- For example: "The current trend is for parents to buy entertaining multi-functional toys for their children in order to free up more time for themselves."

3.5.   Threats

Threats include competitors, new technology that eliminates the need for your product, or government regulations that outlaw your type of product. Note that in some cases, threats can exist now or be realized in months or years to come.

- Name threats in each market segment and note how credible the threat is to your product or business. In addition, name possible substitution products that may replace the need for your product.
- Examples include: "A major competitor is negotiating to purchase a key distribution company, that will make it difficult to sell our product through distribution."

3.6.   Market Drivers

Market drivers are industry norms (generally accepted or officially stated) that consumers and businesses expect when buying a product.

- Name the key issues important in each of your market segments.
- Examples include: "Packaging must be bright and colorful. Advertising must be aimed at both the children and parents. Distribution through Company X is required."

3.7.   Industry Influencers

Industry influencers are people, companies, and agencies that influence purchase decisions. They include industry analysts, magazine product reviews, regulatory agencies, news agencies, or famous individuals.

- Name the industry influencers in each of your market segments.
- For example: "Before buying toys, people read *Consumer Reports* and *Yahoo Groups* on the Internet."

4. Customer

Understanding your prospective customer's world allows you to develop products that fit their needs. This allows you to create marketing and sales campaigns that will grab attention and motivate buying decisions.

4.1. Customer Characteristics

Customers are individual consumers, organizations, or both. Their characteristics are expressed in terms of demographics and psychographics. Demographics include age, sex, income, education, and occupation. Psychographics include lifestyle, personality, religion, and social class.

- Name the demographics and psychographics of a typical customer in each potential market segment. In addition, name the characteristics of a secondary customer type.
- For example: "The end-user of our TurboX are male children, ages five to ten who live in the suburbs of cities with populations over 50,000."

4.2. Customer Decision-Makers and Influencers

Decision-makers and influencers are people who directly influence the purchase decision of a potential customer. These people should be addressed in your marketing and sales strategies and tactics. They include the head of household, purchasing manager, chief financial officer, sales manager, and retail salesperson.

- Name the decision-makers and influencers in each potential market segment.
- For example: "The decision-makers for the TurboX are parents, while influencers are retail store salespeople, friends, and the child."

4.3.   Customer Buying Criteria

People select a product for its ability to solve a problem, satisfy needs and wants, price, value, availability, brand name and style.

- Describe what customers would expect from your product.
- For example: "The customer for the TurboX wants bright colors, rugged design, interchangeable parts, ease of use, low price, and at least a one-year warranty."

4.4.   Customer Buying Process

We all go through a process to select a product. We determine some important buying criteria, gather information, select possible product candidates, and make a purchase. Customers in each market segment have a certain buying process. This might be a determining factor in deciding your target market.

- List the steps customers would go through to buy your type of product. Determine how they'd gather information, how they'd become aware of your product, where they'd look for it, who they'd talk to, how they'd make the final buying decision, and what form of payment they'd prefer.
- For example: "When a five to ten year old child sees an advertisement for a TurboX, he tells his parents that he wants one. If the parents agree, the child and parent(s) go to a toy store to look at the toy. The parent checks for safety information, compares prices to similar products, and asks the salesperson questions."

5.   Goals and Objectives

Now that you understand the market and the behavior of customers in those markets, you'll need to set clear, winnable goals. Goals are specific, measurable, and have a due date. Typical goals include revenue, profit, and market share.

- Name the goals and objectives for your product.
- For example: "Product revenue must be $3 million after the first year of introduction, and $5 million in the second year." Or, "After the first year, TurboX will have a 25% market share of the male children toy market."

6.   Strategies

Once market research is performed and potential customers are understood, it's time to develop strategies to meet the goals and objectives of your product. A strategy is a description of what you'll want and how you'll get it. Create strategies for each of the following:

6.1.   Target Market

A target market offers the most opportunities and least amount of threats. Initially, your target market may not be clear. In this case, you may try to go after a few market segments and see how many customers you'll attract. Keep in mind that it becomes costly and inefficient to go after customers in too many market segments. So, after launching your product, review revenue and expenses from each segment of customers, and then focus just on the most profitable segment.

- Select a target market that's the most profitable, offers the most opportunities, and has the least amount of threats.
- For example, "Our target market consists of married adults between the ages of 25 to 45, owns a small business, and uses the Internet to purchase toys for their children."

6.2.   Product Strategy

A product strategy is the key benefits, features, and functions that your product must have to generate sustainable sales. It includes a timeline of when the product is available, as well as any up-grades, accessories, and future spin-off products. It includes a statement about using continuous improvement or leapfrog technology to improve the product's value and keep ahead of the competition.

- Name your product strategy.
- For example, "TurboX will launch September 2005. It's made with the best materials to withstand temperature extremes, vibration, and moisture. It has an advantage over the competition by offering interchangeable parts that allow the customer to customize the features. Accessories to enhance the colors will be available two months after product launch."

6.2.1. Positioning

Positioning is how you want your product perceived in the marketplace as compared to the competition. Perceptions include the most expensive, the least expensive, the best value, the market leader, the most dependable, the most convenient, the easiest to use, the most comfortable, and so on.

- Describe how you'll want your product perceived.
- For example: "TurboX is positioned as the most enjoyable, toughest, and safest children's product."

6.2.2. Value Proposition

A value proposition is a statement of the value your product adds to your customer's business (for business products) or improves a personal lifestyle (for consumer products).

- Describe the value your product adds. Think from your customer's point of view because they'll ask "What's in it for me?" when considering your product.
- For example, "TurboX provides hours of entertainment value at one-third the price of going to the movies."

6.3. Pricing Strategy

A pricing strategy is determining what customers are willing to pay that's sufficient to meet your revenue or profit goals. Pricing is based on factors such as what the market will bear, cost plus a profit margin, positioning strategy, and competitive comparison. Pricing strategy also depends on market conditions, channel discounts, sales commissions, and your goals and objectives.

- Describe the retail price, channel price, and any discounts.
- For example, "The price is set to 10% above unit costs." Or, "A price point that provides us a 30% margin and a 40% margin to distributors and retailers." Or, "A price that's 5% below comparable competition."

6.4.   Communications Strategy

A communications strategy for your product is the method for raising awareness, producing sales leads, generating interest, and motivating a purchase. Communications include advertising, banner ads, billboards, coupons, direct mail, press releases, press kits, public relations, presentations, special discounts and incentives, partner programs, and trade shows.

- Determine the communications needed to create product awareness, generate leads, and motivate a purchase.
- For example, "Two months before product launch, half-page ads will be placed in trade magazines. On the product launch date a press release will be sent out using Businesswire. Press releases will be issued monthly based on product announcements and new business relationships. Additional leads will be generated from email lists purchased from trade magazines. All leads will be followed-up with an email and phone call."

6.5.   Sales Strategy   *24 hours a 3+ days*

A sales strategy is the method to sell and distribute your product. Methods include field sales, inbound direct response telesales, outbound cold-calling, web-selling, and word-of-mouth referrals. Usually, a combination of these methods is generally most effective.

- Describe the sales method for your product.
- For example, "Trade magazine ads are used to create awareness and direct response leads. The leads are followed up with a telesales person for qualification. Qualified leads are handled by an account representative who takes a consultative approach to look for sales opportunities. A purchase order is received and the product is shipped from a warehouse with 30-day terms."

6.6.   Distribution Strategy

A distribution strategy is the method for getting your product to the customer and for getting paid. Getting your product to a customer includes shipping your product to a distribution center, direct to a retailer, or downloading a file from a website. Methods of getting paid include credit card, check, cash, or purchase order with credit terms.

- Describe the distribution method and names of distributors needed for your product.
- For example, "The product is available for download from our website. The user makes a selection, adds the product to a shopping cart, and then checks out. A credit card is entered, verified, and the amount is deposited to the business checking account. The user is presented with download instructions and gets a thank-you message upon completion."

6.7.   Product Support Strategy

A product support strategy is the method to address customer service needs before and after the sale. It includes the required levels of support such as tier one, two, and three. It includes how customers will contact you, such as an 800 number, email, or a combination of these. The strategy outlines information systems and response times needed to satisfy customers.

- Describe the support required for your product.
- For example, "Initial support contact is handled by email. An automated response is emailed to the sender to inform them that their query was received. A support person attempts to ratify the issue within twenty-four hours. If the issue cannot be resolved, the issue is routed to a manager for determination of a response."

6.8.   Partnership Strategy

Partnerships may or may not be appropriate for you. Partnering is used to offer a complete customer solution, provide access to certain distribution channels, and strengthen perception in the market. Partners include suppliers, industry analysts, agencies, key customer accounts, and companies that offer complementary products or services.

- Determine which organizations you'll need to partner with.
- For example, "Partnering with ToyMax provides a key distribution channel for TurboX."

7.   Tactics by Sales Cycle

Tactics are the action programs that bring the above strategies to life. Each tactical program costs something. Determine the total amount you're willing to spend on marketing and sales. Then, create action programs, and allocate a dollar amount to each item as shown in the following examples. The **Market-Step** Product Plan arranges the tactics by stages of the customer buying process:

1. Awareness and Lead Generation
2. Customer Interest
3. Sales
4. Customer Support

7.1.   Awareness and Lead Generation

To generate a sale, customers must first become aware of your product. Tactics include advertising, promotions, direct mail, press releases, product reviews, trade shows, and your website. The following is a sample action plan to generate awareness and sales leads.

Awareness and Lead Generation Programs		
Programs	**Actions**	**Cost**
Advertising	• Place ads in magazines A, B, C on a monthly basis	$20,000
Direct Mail	• Mail to target organizations within the region	$10,000
Press Releases	• Product launch • Partner relationships • New technology	$8,000
Product Reviews	• Get product reviews in magazines that cover the target market	$ 500
Promotion	• Contests • Premiums • Discounts	$1,500
Trade Shows	• Participate in spring and fall trade shows • Look into partner programs (shared booths, shared pre-show mailings, etc)	$25,000
Web	• Post product information and enable download of brochure when the prospect provides contact information • Exchange links with vendors and distributors • Get placement in search engines • Buy keywords on Google	$10,000
TOTAL		**$ 75,000**

7.2.   Customer Interest

The second step in the sales cycle involves generating real interest in your product. Tactics include free samples, free trial periods, information seminars, partner programs, incentives to distributors, and incentives to retailers. The following is a sample action plan to generate interest.

Customer Interest Programs		
Programs	**Actions**	**Cost**
Prospect Evaluation	• Provide free trial period and free shipping	$5,000
Distributors	• Send product samples • Join their partner program	$5,000
Reference accounts	• Contact major customers to build reference accounts • Solicit testimonials	$5,000
Partnering	• Setup annual user conferences and annual sales meetings	$10,000
TOTAL		**$ 25,000**

7.3.   Sales

Now that you've generated awareness and interest, the third step involves prospecting your potential customers. The objective involves uncovering problems, needs, or wants that your product can solve. Tactics include inside telesales, Internet sales, and face-to-face field sales. The following is a sample action plan to produce sales.

Sales Programs		
Programs	**Actions**	**Cost**
Outside Sales	• Follow-up strong leads • Build relationships • Close sales	$50,000

Inside Sales	• Take incoming calls • Make outbound follow-up calls to direct mail responses and leads from advertisements, web, and trade shows	$20,000
Distributors	• Produce a distributor kit: ordering info, price list, brochures, competitive information	$10,000
TOTAL		**$ 80,000**

7.4.   Customer Support

Customer support is often needed after the sale to help with installation, general use, and customer satisfaction. In addition, customer support is useful before the sale to help with a customer's technical issues. Programs include training for Customer Support staff, setting up a call-tracking database, and periodically assessing customer satisfaction. The following is a sample action plan to facilitate customer support.

Customer Support Programs		
Programs	**Actions**	**Cost**
Sales and Support Training	• Produce training for sales and support staff	$20,000
Systems	• Call-tracking database • Customer satisfaction surveys	$50,000
TOTAL		**$ 70,000**

TOTAL MARKETING AND SALES EXPENSE   **$ 250,000**

8. Profit Summary

Provide a forecast of future sales, cost of goods sold, gross profit, marketing and sales expenses, and net profit. Use a spreadsheet to perform profit forecast calculations and place the results in this section. The following is a sample Profit and Loss statement.

Profit and Loss Statement	
Sales Revenue	3,250,000
Cost of Goods Sold	(2,000,000)
Gross Profit	1,250,000
Operating Expenses:	
Marketing and Sales	250,000
Salaries	200,000
Administrative	50,000
Total Operating Expense	(500,000)
Net Profit Before Taxes	750,000

9. Monitor and Evaluation

Your product plan should outline how you'll monitor your progress. You'll need a procedure of regularly examining your product's progress and making course corrections as needed. Initially, you may do this on a weekly basis, and then as the product matures, on a monthly basis.

9.1. Marketing and Sales Effectiveness

Monitoring marketing effectiveness is measuring the success of your marketing programs. Show how you'll track sales leads from each marketing program and then analyze success.

- Describe what marketing and sales statistics you'll need to monitor on a weekly and monthly basis. Use a spreadsheet and look for trends.

- For example, "The number of leads from advertisements, direct mail, website visitors, and those that generate purchases will be tracked on a weekly basis."

9.2.   Sales Win / Loss Analyses

Sales win / loss analyses are interviews with customers and prospects to determine why you won and lost sales. You can ask customers why they purchased your product. And, ask lost customers why they did not buy your product. Use the feedback to enhance your product, marketing and sales strategies, and tactics.

- Describe how you will monitor your sales progress.
- For example, "New customers will be called one month after a purchase to determine the underlying reasons why they made a purchase. Also, prospects who decided not to buy, will be called on a monthly basis to find out why."

9.3.   Customer Satisfaction

You'll need to monitor customer satisfaction. It's often the case that people complain among themselves but only a small percentage present problems to the company they bought the product from.

- Describe how you'll be proactive in seeking what product features are working and not working. Use the feedback to enhance your product, marketing, and sales strategies and tactics.
- For example, "New customers will be called two weeks after a purchase to discuss ease of installing and getting up to speed. In addition, they'll be called two months after purchase to discuss product satisfaction. Customers will be asked about product quality and their likes and dislikes about the product. In addition, they will be asked for suggestions and comments."

9.4.   Competition Review

Competitors might make changes as a result of your new product. They might change their price, increase marketing, or do nothing at all.

- Describe how you'll monitor activities of current and potential competitors.
- For example, "Competition will be reviewed on a monthly basis. The competitor's press releases, advertising, promotions, sales methods, and changes to pricing will be examined."

Product Plan Notes

The technically superior product does not always win. Winners are good products that are supported by the best marketing and sales systems. In your product plan, describe the way your customer thinks, buys, and makes decisions. Clearly identify how your product meets a need and how to overcome competition. Then, discuss the strategies and tactics to acquire new customers and maintain satisfaction.

Appendix D
Product Math

During the early phases of development you'll need to determine your product's financial viability. And later, if you work with distributors and retailers, you'll need to discuss pricing. Review the following formulas that might apply to your situation.

Profit and Loss

Profit and Loss is an accounting income statement that shows how well your product performed or a forecast of how it might perform over a month, a quarter, or a year. Essentially, profit is revenue minus expenses for a time period. The following is a general list of items to consider as you determine your business profit or loss.

Revenue
- Product Sales
- Maintenance and Support revenue
- Licensing Revenue

Expenses
- Cost of Goods Sold
- Sales and Marketing
- Administrative and Support
- Salary and Benefits
- Consulting
- Office and Supplies
- Miscellaneous Expenses

The general format of a profit and loss statement for a given time period is the following:

Profit and Loss Statement	
Sales Revenue	50,000
Cost of Goods Sold	(10,000)
Gross Profit	40,000
Operating Expenses:	
Marketing and Sales	10,000
Salaries	10,000
Administrative	3,000
Total Operating Expense	(23,000)
Net Profit Before Taxes	17,000

Gross Profit = Sales Revenue – Cost of Goods Sold
Net Profit = Gross Profit – Operating Expenses

Return on Investment

Return on Investment (ROI) is a quick measure of the financial gain versus an amount invested over a time period. This measure is used for projecting future results or determining actual results. For new products, the investment includes the development, marketing, sales, production, administrative, salary, and office expenses. You may also want to consider opportunity costs such as the income you're foregoing while working on your invention. By calculating an ROI, you can determine if proceeding with development makes sense.

ROI should be higher than a risk-free investment such as a Treasury Bill, certificate of deposit, or money market fund. If the ROI for your product is less than the return from investing in a standard certificate of deposit, for example, then it's probably not worth developing the product. On the other hand, if you obtain funding from investors, they will expect a certain ROI for their risk. The following is a simple ROI formula:

$$ROI = \frac{Revenue - Investment}{Revenue}$$

For example, your expected sales revenue for the first year will be $170,000 and your investment will be $150,000.

ROI = ($170,000 – $150,000) / $170,000 = $20,000 / $170,000 = 11%

Therefore, 11% is your product's return on investment. Compare this to a financial risk-free indicator such as a certificate of deposit for the same time period.

Break Even

Break Even is the number of product units you'll need to sell so that revenue equals costs. This is a handy number for determining a minimum sales volume needed to begin making a profit. The formula uses fixed costs that do not vary with sales volume (e.g., rent, utilities, salaries). The formula also uses variable costs such as those needed to produce each product (e.g., materials, packaging, sales commissions). Units sold above this number represent your profit.

$$Break\ Even = \frac{Fixed\ Costs}{Selling\ Price - Variable\ Costs}$$

For example, total fixed costs per month are $10,000, your product has a selling price of $50, and the variable costs to produce each product comes to $10.

Break Even = $10,000 / ($50 - $10) = 250 units

Margins and Discounts

In terms of selling products, margin is the percentage of profit between cost and selling price. The following are a few scenarios when working with distributors and retailers.

Determine a Selling Price

In this scenario you're selling directly to a retailer. You'll need to set a retail price and margin, which will determine and retailer's cost. Use the formula:

$$\text{Retailer's Cost} = \frac{\text{Retail Price}}{1 + \text{Retailer Margin}}$$

For example, you determine a retail price of $19.95, and the retailer wants a margin of 40%.

Retailer's Cost = $19.95 / (1 + .40) = $19.95 / (1.4) = $14.25

Therefore, the retailer's cost (your selling price) is $14.25.

Your Maximum Costs

In this scenario you're selling to a distributor who then sells to a retailer. You'll want to determine the maximum cost of manufacturing your product so that everyone (retailer, distributor, and you) can make a profit. If your costs are too high, it won't make sense financially to develop your product. At the same time, if your costs are too high to go through a distribution channel, you'll need to consider selling direct to end-users.

Let's consider an example where we have a retail price in mind, and we want to determine the distributor cost, retail cost, and your maximum product cost. To do this, we'll work backwards from the retail price.

$$\text{Retailer's Cost} = \frac{\text{Retail Price}}{1 + \text{Retailer Margin}}$$

For example, the Retail Price is $19.95 and the Retailer Margin is 40%. Therefore,

Retailer's Cost = $19.95 / (1 + .40) = $14.25

This means that the retailer will need to buy the product at no higher than $14.25.

If you sell through a distributor, who then sells to a retailer, there's an additional layer of pricing. Let's assume that a distributor also wants a 40% margin. Use the formula:

$$\text{Distributor's Cost} = \frac{\text{Distributor Selling Price}}{1 + \text{Distributor Margin}}$$

Note that the Distributor Selling Price is the same as the Retailer's Cost.

Distributor's Cost = $14.25 / (1+ .40) = $10.18

Therefore, $10.18 is the Distributor's Cost and also your selling price.

$$\text{Your Cost} = \frac{\text{Your Selling Price}}{1 + \text{Your Margin}}$$

To determine if you can make a profit, set a profit margin to cover your costs and room for a net profit. A profit margin should be an amount to cover your costs such as administrative, marketing, selling, and taxes. Check with an accountant to find out the typical profit margin for your type of business. You can also search the Internet for standard business ratios, which will include statistics on typical profit margins.

For example, with a Selling Price of $10.18, and by setting a profit margin of 30%, your cost is $7.83.

Your Cost = $10.18 / (1+ .30) = $7.83

To summarize the example:

Retail Price	$ 19.95
Retailer Cost	$ 14.25
Distributor Cost	$ 10.18
Your Cost	$ 7.83

This means that for everyone to make a profit, your unit product costs can be no higher than $7.83. This number represents your manufacturing cost, packaging, inventory, and other costs related to producing your finished product.

Determine a Profit Margin

From an accounting point of view, you should calculate a profit margin. Each industry has a certain profit margin that's typical of a healthy business. Check with an accountant to find out what's typical for your product type. Given your product costs and selling price, therefore:

$$\text{Profit Margin} = \frac{\text{Selling Price} - \text{Product Costs}}{\text{Selling Price}}$$

For example, your cost to produce and package your product is $10, and the selling price is $12.50.

Profit Margin = ($12.50 - $10.00) / $12.50 = 20%

Therefore, each unit sold will produce a 20% margin.

Discounted Pricing

Let's suppose you want to offer a discount pricing structure based on volume purchases. To determine a retail price for a percent discount use the formula:

$$\text{Retail Price} = \text{Retail Price} \times (1 - \text{Discount})$$

The key is to determine at what quantities you'll offer a discount. I like to have discounts based on the ratio of 1:2:5. This means there's a discount at quantity levels such as 10, 20, 50 or 100, 200, 500 units. This ratio repeats itself and may start at any point. But be sure to check that there's still room for a profit at the lowest levels of discount.

For example, your Retail Price is $10 for one product. Discounts are offered in the following structure:

- 30% discount for quantities of 10 to 19:
  Selling Price   = Retail Price x (1 – Discount)
             = $10 x (1-30%)
             = $10 x (.70)
             = $7

- 40% discount for quantities of 20 to 49:
  Selling Price   = Retail Price x (1 – Discount)
             = $10 x (1-40%)
             = $10 x (.60)
             = $6

- 50% discount for quantities of 50 or more:
  Selling Price   = Retail Price x (1 – Discount)
             = $10 x (1-50%)
             = $10 x (.50)
             = $5

At a selling price of $5, your margin should still be enough to generate a profit.

Appendix E
Funding Your Idea

OK, you have a great idea but it'll cost thousands of dollars to finance. Now what? Raising money is a normal part of doing business, especially if you intend to develop, grow, and expand. This section provides an overview of the funding process. I'll introduce the language of funding, showing you who to get money from, how to prepare, and how to find out how investors view you.

The Need for Money

Money allows you to develop, market, and sell your idea. Initially you'll need money for market research, equipment, prototype development, and to file intellectual property. As you get further along in development, you'll need money for employees, consultants, more equipment, supplies, prototypes, and marketing programs. You'll need money for the following:

- Market research
- Prototype development
- Product development
- Patent filing and legal fees
- Product launch
- Management team
- Employees and consultants
- Advertising and promotion
- Computer equipment and software
- Rent
- Utilities
- Supplies
- Taxes

Investors understand that you'll need money since many businesses fail due to undercapitalization. Investors want to know what you're going to do with the money once they give it to you. They'll want to make sure you're clear about how to allocate it properly to develop the business and that you won't be using it to take a vacation. You'll need to show how much you require, what you're going to use it for, how long the money will last, and how much revenue you'll generate.

How much money will you need? You'll need to realistically estimate what you'll need to grow your invention. Make a list of everything you'll need and then allocate a dollar amount for each item. Remember that some expenses are one-time events (e.g., marketing reports, equipment to build a prototype, filing for a patent) and others are recurring (e.g., office rent, utilities, salary). Calculate the total expenses needed for the first and second years.

Types of Funding

Funding basically comes in two flavors: debt and equity. Debt is money you borrow and pay back; equity involves giving up partial ownership in exchange for money.

- **Debt** – Debt funding is a loan that you must repay. Typically, lines of credit are used for working capital and term loans are used to buy fixed assets. The typical term of a loan can be from one to ten years. And the start of repayment can begin the following month or the following year. When you meet with a lender, the loan officer will create a reasonable repayment plan.
- **Equity** – Equity funding involves selling a part of the business in exchange for money. This is accomplished by forming a corporation, then issuing shares of stock to yourself, and then a percentage to your equity investors. Another method of equity financing involves bringing in partners for partial ownership in exchange for money and expertise.

The Investors

In general, you should seek investors according to what stage your business is at and how much money you need. Money can be acquired from a variety of sources. Your initial source of funding will most likely come from friends and family. Other sources include Angel Investors, Venture Capitalists, Investment Bankers, and Investment Brokers. But before asking for funding, you'll need to show that you have a viable product idea and a viable business that will grow.

- **Friends and Family (debt and equity)** – It might be risky to infringe upon personal relationships, but friends and family are sources of funding. You have to consider what will happen to the relationship if you lose the money they invested. Some of your friends and family can probably afford to gamble a few thousand dollars here and there. You'll need to determine whether they want to invest with a loan or with equity and become partial owners. Equity investors will need to receive a written agreement stating the number of shares of stock they've been issued. Debt investors will need a written agreement that includes repayment terms.

- **Angel Investors (equity)** – Angels are typically wealthy individuals acting alone or pooling their money in an investment group. Instead of going to Las Vegas to gamble, they risk funding new businesses with the expectation of a high return. Angels are usually business people who have made enough to retire but are still interested in the excitement of business.

  Angels are usually only comfortable investing in a certain type of technology or market. You'll need to find Angels who specialize in your type of product industry. Angels who operate individually may invest from $50,000 to $250,000. On the other hand, a pooled group of Angels may invest up to $3 million. The amount they will fund is usually enough to carry your business for one to two years. But before Angels provide funding, they'll perform due diligence on you and your idea. In exchange for their investment, Angels receive a percent equity ownership in your business. And in five to seven years after handing over the funds, Angels hope to recoup from five to ten times the amount they invested.

- **Venture Capitalists (equity)** – Venture Capitalists are managers of a fund. Wealthy individuals and organizations put money into the fund hoping for a large return for their risk. In fact, they seek a greater return on investment than what they could normally get in the market over the same time period.

  The Venture Capitalist (VC) manages the fund by investing in new businesses that are willing to give up equity in exchange for money. The goal for the VC is to grow the fund by getting the new business to go public or be acquired. When a new business goes public through an initial public offering (IPO) or is acquired, the proceeds are sold and placed back into the fund. The VC anticipates that an IPO or acquisition will occur in three to seven years. Acquisitions occur more commonly than an IPO.

  VCs provide more than just money. They provide expertise in management, marketing, and have key contacts who may become large customers. The VCs have a vested interest in growing your business. In some cases, depending on your expertise, your role may become minor as new management comes in to run the business. You still have equity in the business and when the business goes public or is acquired, you get cash or publicly traded stock that you can sell.

- **Bankers (debt)** – Bankers help businesses grow by lending money. Bankers perform careful analyses to make sure you can pay off the loan based on your business generating a positive cash flow. Therefore, most Bankers do not fund startups, preferring instead to see a positive track record of revenue and paying your bills in a timely manner.

In almost all cases, Bankers will seek a personal financial guarantee so that you don't take the money and retire to the Cayman Islands. Personal financial guarantees include assets such as real estate, stocks, bonds, and mutual funds. Also, Bankers will loan money when it's backed by the value of your inventory or accounts receivable, but that depends on the Banker. You'll need to understand that Bankers consider many factors before handing over money. Also, keep in mind that Bankers can provide general advice, but they will not get involved in managing your business.

Plan ahead. It can take from six to twelve months from the day you ask for money to the time you receive it. This means you'll need to have cash flow or other investments to keep you afloat during that time period.

Stages of Funding

Whether you intend to market your idea yourself or license it, your need for money will vary according to which stage your business is at. Funding stages include:

- **Seed capital** – Money for initial research and business planning. Seed capital is likely to come from you, friends, family, and Angels.
- **Start-up capital** – Money that pays for rent, market studies, prototype equipment, supplies, etc., for the first year or so of operation. Start-up capital is likely to come from you, friends, family, and Angels.
- **Mezzanine capital** – Money to help your business grow, move to a better office, launch a marketing campaign, or purchase new equipment. Mezzanine capital is likely to come from Bankers and Venture Capitalists.

- **Bridge capital** – Money to bridge the gap between your current funding and the next level of funding. Bridge capital is likely to come from Bankers and Venture Capitalists.

What Type of Funding Do You Go After?

Whether you go after debt or equity funding will depend on your comfort level. Ask yourself a few questions:

Pursue Debt?

- Do I have personal collateral to guarantee the loan?
- Am I willing to lose my collateral such as a house in the event the business fails?
- Can I make the monthly payments to pay off the debt?

Pursue Equity?

- Am I willing to give up some control in exchange for funding?
- Am I willing to take advice from equity investors?
- Am I willing to share the profits?
- Am I willing and able to make a series of presentations to investors to excite them about my idea?

If you're comfortable with loans and have collateral, seek a loan from a bank or from friends and family. If you're lucky enough to know someone who is not adverse to risks and losses, see if they'd lend some money without requiring collateral. Otherwise, equity is your funding route.

To Receive You Must First Give It Up

Who likes the thought of giving up a piece of their business? But, if you want equity funding, that's how the game is played.

On the positive side, the investors know how to grow money, can lend advice, and have key contacts that can lead to customers. I like the phrase: "A rising tide floats all boats." In the context of funding, you make money and your investors make money. Everyone wins.

How much ownership you give up depends on the value of your business and how much an investor contributes. The value of your business today is based on the potential future revenue or profit. The valuation process will be performed by an experienced finance professional.

For example, let's assume your business is valued at $750,000 based on future revenue. And, let's assume you need $250,000 from an equity investor. A $250,000 investment plus the original value of $750,000 creates a new business value of $1,000,000. Ownership is a percentage of investment to the total value. Your ownership is $750,000 divided by $1,000,000 or 75%. And, the investor's ownership is $250,000 divided by $1,000,000 or 25%.

Business Value After Funding		
	Before Funding	**After Funding**
1. Business value: 2. Investor adds: 3. New value:	$ 750,000	$ 250,000 $1,000,000
Your ownership %: Your ownership $:	100% $ 750,000	75% $ 750,000
Investor's ownership %: Investor's ownership $:		25% $ 250,000

As you can see by this example, receiving equity funding decreases the percentage of your ownership. However, your dollar ownership remains the same after the investment and will grow as the value of the business grows.

This example is a simplification, but it's the general approach for determining percent ownership. In addition, each time you seek more funding, your percent ownership decreases. But, as market conditions change, the value of the business changes – up and down. The good news is that as more money comes into your business from investors and customers, the value of your business increases. So, even though your percent ownership decreases, your dollar value should increase. Don't be afraid to give up equity, it could lead to more for you.

Prepare for Funding

You'll need to do some homework before seeking equity or debt funding. Two key activities involve creating a business plan and forming a management team.

Initially, while you're exploring your invention's market-ability, the business entity can be just a sole proprietorship. Then, once you believe the market is viable, form a corporation. In general, if you're seeking equity investors, consider forming a C-corporation so that you can issue shares of ownership. You may not think you want equity investors now, but that may change later. Check with a business attorney about what makes sense in the long term.

At some point you'll need a management team, but you may start with advisors. You'll need an advisory team for guidance and to show investors that you have people to provide leadership in every aspect of your business. Ideally, the advisory team includes a technical person, a financial person, a legal person, and a marketing strategy person. In addition to being competent in their fields, advisors should be able to introduce you to key customers, distributors, or suppliers. The team is comprised of people you know personally, or are referred to you. Together, they form the core of your business and help you brainstorm strategies and tactics.

Your advisory team might want to get paid up front or might ask for a small percentage of the business in the form of stock options. Later, when you get funding, hire the advisors as full-time management, or hire new managers and keep the advisors as consultants or board members. The advisors may take either a less active role in managing and assume a general oversight role, or participate on your board of directors.

Steps to Get Funding

Billions of dollars are invested in businesses like yours every year. Obtaining funding will take persistence and determination. Follow these steps and you're on your way:

1. Determine the marketability and feasibility of your idea
2. Form an advisory team
3. Make a list of your funding needs and a dollar amount
4. Form a business entity
5. Determine what type of funding you want
6. Understand what investors want
7. Write a business plan to entice investors
8. Contact investors and form a business relationship
9. Submit a proposal
10. Negotiate terms of funding

When Do You Seek Funding?

When you want funding, investors like to see that you are prepared. Here are a few tips about approaching investors:

- Invest some of your own money in prototype development or marketing research. Since investors are taking a risk, they like to see you take a risk as well.
- If possible, show you already have interested customers through sales or feedback from surveys or beta tests. Investors like to see validation of your idea by others.

- File any patent, trademark, or copyright applications. Investors like to see intellectual property, which adds business value.
- Approach investors when a business plan is complete. Investors like to see that you've done your homework.
- Have a business entity in place such as a C-corporation. Investors fund businesses rather than an individual.

The Investor's Process

Investors proceed with caution, even if they like you and your idea. You'll need to prove your case before they open up their checkbook. Investors will typically first review a proposal consisting of an introductory letter and business plan executive summary. If they like the proposal, investors will:

1. Evaluate your business plan
2. Perform due diligence on you and the viability of the product idea and business concept
3. Have you make a presentation
4. Make an investment decision
5. Structure a funding plan
6. Provide your business with the money

How Investors Evaluate You and Your Idea

Being a credible person is as important as having a great idea. Investors will judge you and everyone involved on character. You must have a reputation as honest and respectable in your personal and business life. You must honor your commitments and deliver more than you promise. Investors will look at your credit history, including your ability to pay on time, bankruptcies, liens, as well as lawsuits.

To ask for funding, you'll need a solid business plan showing how your product will make a profit, how you'll grow the business, how you're able to manage the business, and how you'll pay off investors. Business plan formats vary, but the following format will satisfy most investors:

1. Cover Letter
2. Executive Summary
   a. The Market
   b. The Business Model
   c. The Management
   d. The Money
3. The Company
4. Mission Statement
5. Management
6. The Opportunity
7. Products and Markets
8. Sales and Profit Summary
9. Funding Requirements
10. Investment Proposal

Investors will evaluate your business plan based on Market, Business Model, Management, and Money. Investors want to know:

The Market

- Is there a market for your product?
- Who is the target market and what are the demographics of the customers?
- For a business buyer, what's the benefit of your product (e.g., lower costs, higher revenue, higher margins, increased customer retention)?
- For a consumer buyer, what's the benefit of your product (e.g., better health, lower costs, prestige, fun to use, saves time)?
- Is there an exciting and significant market for your product (e.g., new trends, high growth, capitalize on new technologies)?

- What are the advantages of your product over the competition? How will you sustain the advantages and create new advantages?
- Do you have access to distribution channels?

The Business Model

- What is the business model and how will you grow the business (e.g., licensing your idea to a manufacturer, selling your product to a retail chain, collecting monthly subscription fees)?
- Is there a compelling, well-articulated strategy for capturing and defending a significant market share?
- Is there proprietary technology or other strong barriers to entry?

The Management

- Does the management team have experience and can they execute their plan (e.g., experience in the industry, grew a similar business before, has a proven record)?
- Are you open to advice and coaching?

The Money

- What are the product costs and selling price?
- How many units will you sell the first year?
- When will the business be profitable?
- How much money do you need?
- Once you receive funding, how will you use the money (e.g., R&D, marketing, administration)?
- Equity investors want to know: What's the exit strategy for investors (e.g., acquired by a competitor, acquired by a company offering complementary products, or taking your business public)?

Funding Rejection

Equity investors will reject funding proposals that are not thoroughly and properly prepared. Here are some common reasons for rejection:

- The business plan is poorly written. It was not written with an investor as the intended audience.
- The business has only a small growth potential. Many equity investors want to see at least a 20% to 50% return above the current rate of a safe investment such as a Treasury bond or certificate of deposit.
- Investors do not understand your product idea or your industry.
- You do not have enough experience. Investors want to see that you have industry experience. They also want to see experience owning a business, or being involved in managing a business.
- Lack of commitment. Investors want to see that you're fully committed to developing your idea and generating revenue. Also, they prefer that you've invested some of your own money.
- Difficult to protect your idea. Investors want to know that your idea cannot be easily copied by existing or new competition. They prefer something that is hard to duplicate, or legally protected with patents, trademarks, or copyrights.

Debt lenders are primarily concerned about repayment. The lending officer will consider the following:

- Have you invested savings or personal equity in your business that's at least 25% to 50% of the loan you're requesting? A lender will not finance 100% of your business.

- Do you have a sound record of creditworthiness as indicated by your credit report, work history, and letters of recommendation?
- Do you have sufficient experience and training to operate a successful business?
- Does the business have sufficient cash flow to make the monthly payments?

SBA Loans

The Small Business Administration (SBA) does not provide loans, but will guarantee a percentage of a loan made by a bank or investment company. Lenders like this because the SBA will cover a percentage of the loss in the form of unpaid interest if you can't pay back a loan. But just because the SBA will cover a loss, doesn't mean a lender will be less stringent evaluating you and your business.

SBA loan programs are generally intended to encourage longer term small business financing, but the actual loan maturity is based on the ability to repay and the purpose of the loan. In addition, short-term loans are also available through the SBA to help small businesses meet their working capital needs.

For an SBA-backed loan, seek an SBA lender in your area. Contact them to find out what's involved with getting a loan. Be sure to ask what types of SBA loans are available. There are three types of approved SBA lenders:

- **Preferred lenders** – They can make a final decision without SBA approval, which means approval time is quicker than for other types of SBA lenders.
- **Certified lenders** – They need the SBA to make the final decision, which means the approval process is longer.
- **Participant lenders** – They rarely make SBA loans.

The SBA website lists certified and preferred lenders. (www.sba.gov/gopher/Local-Information/Certified-Preferred-Lenders/)

Other Funding Possibilities

I've included some other interesting forms of funding. They might be appropriate if your business is already generating revenue but needs additional funding.

- **Factoring** – Factoring involves an exchange of your accounts receivables for funding. Think of this as a stepping stone before qualifying for a traditional bank loan. With factoring, you're essentially selling your receivables at a discount so you can get cash now rather than waiting for customers to pay you. Private organizations that offer this service are responsible for all collections and may charge from 2% to 10% based on the amount they collect.
- **Purchase Order Advances** – Purchase Order Advances are similar to factoring except that you're trading your customer purchase order asset to gain some funding. This type of funding usually has high rates, so use it judiciously.
- **Convertible Debt** – Convertible Debt is a loan that can convert to equity instead of paying back the loan. You can usually get a better interest rate with convertible debt, but you'll need to make sure that giving up equity is right for you.
- **Limited Partnerships** – Limited Partnerships allow you to take on partners who'll invest money without being liable for losses other than their original investment. You bear all of the financial risk, but you maintain full control. Check with state laws and an attorney before pursuing this.
- **Private Placement** – Private Placement involves offering stock in your business privately without going through an intermediary or registering your company under Federal securities laws. Private Placement takes the form of equity, secured promissory notes, or limited

partnerships. Check with state laws, an attorney, or CPA before pursuing this.

Additional Funding Tips

Here are some more tips that may help you get funding for your invention:

- If you're a woman or a minority, look into the various business grants and loans available.
- If your partner is a woman or minority, consider transferring the primary business ownership to qualify for special grants and loans.
- Look for grants and loans funded by your county and city government. There are often programs available to stimulate the local economy.
- Build credibility by seeking a small loan and then paying it off in a timely manner.
- Get your business plan reviewed before submitting it to an investor. Ask a local businessperson, a college professor, or a business consultant to provide comments.
- If you need someone to write a business plan and you're short on funds, try trading your skills for theirs.

Funding Resources

Resources for funding include:

Angel Capital Electronic Network (ACE-Net)
An investor network sponsored by the SBA
(www.sba.gov/financing/acenet.html)

Small Business Investment Company Program (SBIC)
Investment firms licensed by the SBA
(www.sba.gov/financing/investment.html)

Tech Coast Angels
California angel group
(www.techcoastangels.com)

Global Financial Network
A financial search engine
(www.cfol.com)

BusinessFinance.com
A source for funding options
(www.businessfinance.com)

StartUpBiz.com
Business information
(www.startupbiz.com)

Tatum CFO
Business financial advice
(www.tatumcfo.com)

Housing and Urban Development
Assistance to small and disadvantaged businesses to sell products and services to the government
(www.hud.gov/groups/smallbusiness.cfm)

Appendix F
Business Startup

Launching a product requires setting up and maintaining a business. Your business involves developing and marketing your product, raising money, generating a cash flow, following rules and regulations, and paying taxes. Legally, your business must be a certain type of business entity.

Business Entity Advantages and Disadvantages

Select the type of business entity that will limit your liability, reduce taxes, is structured toward raising money, and is easy to set up. You may choose from a number of legal business entities. In the early stages, as you research your idea's marketability, I suggest keeping your costs low by operating as a sole proprietorship. Then, when you seek funding or are about to produce your product, form a corporation. Here are the advantages and disadvantages of different types of business entities.

Sole Proprietorship

A sole proprietorship is the easiest form of business to set up and maintain. Legally, your business and personal assets are one and the same. Profit or loss generated by the business gets reported on Schedule C or F of your personal tax return. You can run the business either as an individual or as a married couple. In addition, you're allowed to hire employees, but I suggest having work performed by independent consultants or a contracting agency in the beginning. If you hire employees you'll need to get a tax ID number, set up a payroll system, and pay additional taxes.

Advantages:
- Very little paperwork
- Business losses can be deducted from your personal income to reduce your overall tax obligation
- You have full control over the business

Disadvantages:
- No liability protection, which means that if your business is sued, losses can be deducted from the business and your personal assets (but you can buy liability insurance, which is explained in the next section)
- Any debts are repaid from business and personal holdings
- Raising money may be more difficult

General Partnership

A general partnership is an agreement between two or more people who share ownership of a business. They share profits and losses according to their percentage of participation. From a tax perspective, each partner's share of profit or loss is reported on Schedule E of your personal tax return. If you start a partnership, I suggest creating a partnership agreement where you clearly spell out duties, responsibilities, and an exit clause.

Advantages:
- Easy method of forming a business for two or more people
- Business losses can be deducted from your personal income to reduce your overall tax obligation

Disadvantages:
- Each partner is held personally liable for all claims, debts, and taxes against the partnership
- Insurance is needed in the event one partner dies
- Duties and responsibilities of each partner are not always maintained

Limited Liability Partnership

A Limited Liability Partnership operates similarly to a General Partnership except there are both general partners and limited partners. A limited partner is an investor but cannot participate in managing the business. In the event of a financial loss sustained by a business, the limited partner is limited to the amount invested. But if a limited partner participates in business management decisions, the limited partner is then treated as a general partner and responsible for all losses.

Corporation

There are C-corporations, S-corporations, and Professional Corporations. A corporation is comprised of shareholders, directors, and officers. The shareholders are the owners who elect a board of directors to oversee the business. Then, the board of directors hires officers such as the president and vice presidents to manage the business. This may sound like a lot of people, but the shareholders, directors, and officers could consist of just a husband and wife.

Keep in mind that there are public and private corporations. A corporation becomes public when it files with the Securities and Exchange Commission to trade its stock in the market. Your private corporation is held in control without being influenced by the public market.

Articles of Incorporation are filed with the state to form a corporation. Each state has slightly different rules that govern corporations. Talk to a business attorney to discuss the advantages and disadvantages of filing in your home state or another state such as Delaware or Nevada that has certain tax benefits.

C–Corporation

In general, the commonly used term "corporation" is usually a C-corporation. With a C-corporation, any profits that the business earns are taxed at the corporate rate. In addition, any money you take out of the business in the form of salary, bonus, or dividends, is also taxed. This is known as double taxation. Note that you're not required to take a salary, bonus, or declare dividends.

Advantages:
- Liability is generally limited to the assets of the corporation (personal assets are protected)
- It's easier to raise money compared to other business entities in which equity is exchanged for shares of stock
- There can be many classes of stock issued such as common and preferred classes
- There can be an unlimited number of shareholders
- Medical insurance premiums are tax deductible

Disadvantages:
- More paperwork is required than other business entities
- Can be ten times more costly to set up and maintain than a sole proprietorship or partnership
- More regulations to observe
- Double taxation in that the business is taxed at the corporate rate and you pay taxes on your salary, bonus, or any dividends

S–Corporation

A corporation can be set up as a Subchapter S-corporation. An S-corporation has generally the same liability protection as a C-corporation. But the main difference is that profits and losses are reported on your personal income tax return similar to a sole proprietorship or partnership. As a result, there is no corporate tax, dividends to pay out, and no double taxation.

Another difference is that there are limits on the type of stock that an S-corporation can issue. As a result, in some cases this may be a disadvantage when seeking investors.

Advantages:
- No double taxation compared to a C-corporation
- Business losses can be deducted from your personal income to reduce your overall tax obligation

Disadvantages:
- Stock is limited to one class
- There's a limit of 75 shareholders
- Shareholders cannot be a corporation, partnership, or foreign entity
- The limitations on stock may be a problem for investors who may want to take the company public later

Professional Corporation

If the business consists primarily of professional services, regulations require the corporation be formed as a Professional Corporation. Professional services include accounting, architecture, finance, legal, and medical. Talk to an attorney who has experience setting up a professional corporation in your state. If you're in business primarily to sell products, a Professional Corporation is not applicable to you.

Limited Liability Company (LLC)

An LLC has characteristics of both a corporation and a partnership. Your liability is limited to the assets of the business, which provides you with personal protection. Compared to a corporation, an LLC has members instead of stockholders and membership interests instead of stock. And, members must all be U.S. citizens or resident aliens. The profits and losses of an LLC are shared and reported on your personal income tax return similar to a sole proprietorship, partnership, or S-corporation.

Advantages:
- No double taxation
- Limits on liability are similar to a corporation

- Business losses can be deducted from your personal income to reduce your overall tax obligation

Disadvantages:
- Requires at least two members (some states allow one member)
- Membership interests are limited to one class
- There are a limited number of members which might be a problem if there is a desire to issue membership interests to many investors
- More costly to set up and maintain than a sole proprietorship or partnership

Business Entity Considerations

If you intend to raise money in exchange for stock, you need to know that many investors prefer a C-corporation as opposed to an LLC or S-corporation. If you want the protection of a corporation and are not seeking investors, then an S-corporation is suitable. Remember that you may convert an S-corporation to a C-corporation later.

When you discuss business formation with an attorney, take the following issues into account:

- Setup costs
- Paying taxes
- Limiting your liability
- Protecting your assets
- Continuity of the business in the event of death
- Raising money
- Insurance coverage
- Number of owners
- Amount of paperwork
- Benefits such as medical coverage

Liabilities

The term "liability" covers a range of business matters. Liability means you're responsible for issues that include financial debts, product failure, or a personal injury on the job. As mentioned above, business entity structures such as the C-corporation will shield your personal holdings from business liabilities.

The term "limited liability" means your personal losses will not exceed your investment in the business. For example, if your business is a corporation and is sued, and the losses exceed the available business assets, your personal assets are not at risk. But, you do risk losing whatever money you invested into the business. In general, there are four ways to reduce the risk of liability:

- **Business entity** – Setting up a corporation or a Limited Liability Company provides more liability protection than a sole proprietorship or partnership.
- **Insurance protection** – Your business can be sued for issues such as product liability, personal injury, errors, or omissions. Any fines imposed could be high enough to put you out of business. For protection, there are business insurance plans that can cover a business from losses. Discuss liability in detail with an insurance agent who specializes in business insurance. Note also that some trade shows will require liability insurance before you'll be permitted to set up a booth.
- **Customer waivers and releases** – If you've used a software or web-based product, you probably have come across the need to agree to certain terms before you may use the product. These agreements help reduce company liability. They do not release the company from recklessness or negligence. These waivers and releases mean that in the normal course of using the product there are certain limits of recourse by the customer if there's a problem. Talk with an attorney to see if waivers and releases apply to your product.

- **Product certifications** – Passing regulations or receiving certifications might be required for your product. Whether certifications are required or not, I recommend having an independent test lab check for product issues that could be hazardous to your customer. Identifying and fixing issues before product launch can limit the risk of liability.

Business Startup Checklist

Here's a checklist of activities for starting up your business:

- ❑ Evaluate the marketability of your idea (see "Your Roadmap to Success" in Chapter 2).
- ❑ Determine your funding requirements (see "Funding Your Idea" in Appendix E).
- ❑ Select a name for your business.
- ❑ Write a business plan.
- ❑ Determine the business legal structure (sole proprietorship, partnership, or corporation).
- ❑ Call your City Clerk, County Clerk, or Secretary of State office to determine the requirements for a business license, certification, or permit.
- ❑ If your business is a sole proprietorship or partnership, and operating under a name other than the owner(s) name, then you need to file a "Fictitious Name" also known as a DBA (Doing Business As). Contact your City Clerk or County Clerk for specific instructions.
- ❑ Call the Internal Revenue Service at (866) 816-2065 or visit their website (www.irs.gov) to obtain a federal employer identification number (EIN). An EIN is not needed if you are a sole proprietor without employees.
- ❑ Call your state Board of Equalization or state Department of Treasury to determine the requirements for collecting sales tax.
- ❑ Open a checking account for your business.

❑ If you plan to hire employees, check with the U.S. Department of Labor website (www.dol.gov) to review employee rights. For additional help, contact the Employment Development Department in your state.

❑ To protect the name of your business, contact your Secretary of State to register a service mark (see "Protecting Your Idea" in Chapter 4).

❑ Establish a website and email account.

❑ Order business cards and stationary.

❑ Establish a method to track revenue, expenses, and inventory with a system such as Quicken or QuickBooks, made by Intuit.

❑ Establish a method to track your customers' contact information with a system such as Microsoft Outlook.

Further Startup Guidance

Additional resources for business startup include:

- Federal Trade Commission Business Guidance (www.ftc.gov/ftc/business.htm)
- National Association of Women Business Owners (www.nawbo.org)
- Small Business Administration (www.sba.gov)
- Small Business Development Center (www.sba.gov/sbdc)
- U.S. Chamber of Commerce (www.uschamber.com)

Appendix G
Non-Disclosure Agreement

The following is a sample Non-Disclosure Agreement. It's only provided as a guide and not intended to be legal advice. Have an attorney review all legal documents to provide adequate protection.

Inventor(s) _____ and
Participant(s) _____ agree:

1. The parties have been or expect to engage in discussions about their respective businesses that may involve the disclosure of Confidential Information generally regarding:

_____.

2. "Affiliate" means any other entity that controls, is controlled by, or is under common control of a party hereto.

"Confidential Information" means information obtained by the Receiving Party from the Disclosing Party (including, without limitation, information discovered by the Receiving Party while on the premises of the Disclosing Party) that (a) derives economic value, actual or potential, from not being generally known to or readily ascertainable by other persons who could obtain economic value from its disclosure or use, and (b) is the subject of efforts that are reasonable under the circumstances to maintain its secrecy.

Notwithstanding the foregoing, Confidential Information shall not include any information that the Receiving Party can conclusively show (i) is or becomes available in the public domain through no fault of the Receiving Party; (ii) was in the possession of the Receiving Party before receipt from the Disclosing Party; (iii) is received from a third party that legitimately acquired such information without restrictions as to its use or dissemination; (iv) was independently developed by the Receiving Party; or (v) as may be required by law.

"Disclosing Party" or "Receiving Party" shall mean either party to this Agreement, as the case may be, and shall include any Affiliates of each party.

3. The Receiving Party shall not disclose any Confidential Information to any other person or entity without the prior written consent of the Disclosing Party.

4. The Receiving Party shall exercise at least a reasonable degree of care in safeguarding and protecting the Confidential Information from disclosure or unauthorized use.

5. The Receiving Party shall not copy, reproduce, divulge, publish, or circulate Confidential Information to any of its employees or professional advisors other than those who have a need to know.

6. The term of this Agreement shall be one year and thereafter this Agreement shall automatically be extended for successive one-year terms unless terminated by either party upon written notice.

7. All obligations hereunder shall survive for a period of five years after termination.

8. The Receiving Party shall return to the Disclosing Party all copies of all Confidential Information immediately upon receipt of a request from the Disclosing Party for the return of the Confidential Information.

9. Nothing in this Agreement shall be construed or interpreted as granting any license, copyright, or other interest in or to any Confidential Information. The Disclosing Party shall retain title to all intellectual property and proprietary rights in the Confidential Information.

10. Each party acknowledges that the other party may now market or have under development, products that are competitive with products or services now offered or that may be offered by the other party. Any disclosures pursuant to this Agreement shall not serve to impair the right of either party to independently develop, make, use, procure, or market products or services now or in the future that may be competitive with those offered by the other.

11. This Agreement shall be governed by the laws of the State of

_____.

12. This Agreement may be executed in one or more counterparts, all of which together shall constitute one and the same instrument.

13. Neither party may assign any of its rights or obligations under this Agreement without the prior written consent of the other party, except in connection with a merger or acquisition of all or substantially all of the assets of the assignor. Subject to the foregoing, this Agreement shall endure to the benefit of and bind the successors and assigns of the parties.

IN WITNESS WHEREOF the parties have caused this Agreement to be executed as of the _____ day of the month of _____, in the year _____.

SIGNATURES

Inventor's Name
Address
City, State Zip

Signed: _____

Date: _____

PARTICIPANT(S)

Participant's Name
Address
City, State Zip

Signed: _____

Date: _____

Participant's Name
Address
City, State Zip

Signed: _____

Date: _____

Index

Ordering Information

For information about ordering additional copies of *Product Idea to Product Success*, please visit the Broadword Publishing website (www.Broadword.com). For ordering a book by check or money order, send $24.95 plus $3.85 for priority shipping in the United States ($28.80). Add $2.00 for shipping each additional book. Please make amount payable to Broadword Publishing and mail to:

Broadword Publishing
166 London Court, Dept. A2
Cardiff, NJ 08234

Templates

Templates presented in this book are available on CD or as a download from the author's website (www.MattYubas.com). Templates include:

- Licensing Proposal
- Idea Assessment
- Idea Description
- Similar Products
- Benefits and Features
- Product Advantages
- Revenue Potential
- Cost of Goods Sold
- Expense Estimates
- Profit Potential
- Customer Profile
- Concept Survey
- Product Characteristics
- Patent Search Log
- Prototype Goals
- Prototype Interview Plan
- Marketing Communication Tools
- Distribution Planning
- Marketing Theme
- Packaging Elements
- Packaging Design
- Product Launch Kit
- Marketing and Sales Log
- Competitive Analysis
- Target Market Selection
- Market-Step Product Plan
- Business Startup Checklist

Make Your Idea a Reality

Whether it's a new product idea or service, inventions abound. Coming up with the idea is one thing, getting it to fly is another. In his new book, *Product Idea to Product Success; A Complete Step-by-Step Guide to Making Money from Your Idea,* author Matthew Yubas offers readers a comprehensive, complete, practical, and easy-to-understand guide to the process of bringing an invention to market.

Anyone with a great idea for a new product or service can benefit from this book. In an engaging and conversational style, *Product Idea to Product Success* is filled with examples and real-world advice as Yubas takes readers through a step-by-step process to get from idea to finished product. Yubas even provides a method for determining whether a market exists before investing time and money on a product or service, and then gives readers ways to brainstorm new ideas for future inventions. *Product Idea to Product Success* is an educational and thought-provoking mix of quizzes, surveys, marketing plan formats, and everything else readers will need to launch their ideas.

Yubas fills *Product Idea to Product Success* with sound advice and cost-effective solutions that, if followed carefully, are almost guaranteed to produce success. This book will become a valued guide to new and experienced inventors and entrepreneurs alike.